On the Wing of
a Whitebird

```
J         813.54 Hornburg c.1
Hornburg, Val. Z.
On the wing of a whitebird
a Tomie DePaola resource
```

On the Wing of a Whitebird

A Tomie dePaola Resource Book

VAL Z. HORNBURG

Teacher Ideas Press, an imprint of Libraries Unlimited
Westport, Connecticut • London

Library of Congress Cataloging-in-Publication Data

Hornburg, Val Z.
  On the wing of a whitebird : a Tomie DePaola resource book / by Val Z. Hornburg.
    p. cm.
    ISBN 1–59469–007–3 (alk. paper : pbk.)
    1. De Paola, Tomie—Study and teaching. 2. Children's stories,
American—Study and teaching. 3. Children—Books and reading—United
States. I. Title.
PS3554.E11474Z57   2005
813'.54—dc22   2005047480

British Library Cataloguing in Publication Data is available.

Copyright © 2005 by Val Z. Hornburg

All rights reserved. No part of this book may be reproduced
in any form or by any electronic or mechanical means, including
information storage and retrieval systems, without permission
in writing from the publisher, except by a reviewer, who may
quote brief passages in a review. An exception is made for
individual librarians and educators who may make copies of
portions of the scripts for classroom use. Reproducible pages
may be copied for classroom and educational purposes only.
Performances may be videotaped for school or library purposes.

Library of Congress Catalog Card Number: 2005047480
ISBN: 1–59469–007–3

First published in 2005

Libraries Unlimited/Teacher Ideas Press, 88 Post Road West, Westport, CT 06881
A Member of the Greenwood Publishing Group, Inc.
www.lu.com

Printed in the United States of America

The paper used in this book complies with the
Permanent Paper Standard issued by the National
Information Standards Organization (Z39.48–1984).

10 9 8 7 6 5 4 3 2 1

*For Tomie dePaola, my inspiration,
and Bill and Noelle Zuelke, the loves of my life.*

Contents

Acknowledgments ix

Introduction by Tomie dePaola xi

Introduction by Val Hornburg xiii

Biographical Information about Tomie dePaola xv

How to Use the Literary Guides xvii

Chapter 1 The Autobiographical Stories 1

    Introduction 1

    Andy, That's My Name 1

    Oliver Button Is a Sissy 6

    The Art Lesson 8

    Now One Foot, Now the Other 14

    Tom 20

    Nana Upstairs & Nana Downstairs 22

    Watch Out for the Chicken Feet in Your Soup 25

    The Baby Sister 28

Chapter 2 The *Strega Nona* Series 33

    Introduction 33

    Strega Nona 34

    Big Anthony and the Magic Ring 43

    Strega Nona's Magic Lessons 48

    Merry Christmas, Strega Nona 54

    Strega Nona Meets Her Match 60

Strega Nona: Her Story 65

Big Anthony: His Story 71

Strega Nona Takes a Vacation 74

Chapter 3   The Irish Stories 79

Introduction 79

Fin M'Coul, the Giant of Knockmany Hill 79

Jamie O'Rourke and the Big Potato 88

Jamie O'Rourke and the Pooka 95

Chapter 4   The *Bill and Pete* Stories 101

Introduction 101

Bill and Pete 101

Bill and Pete Go Down the Nile 104

Bill and Pete to the Rescue 107

Chapter 5   A Visit with Tomie dePaola 113

Chapter 6   Celebrating Tomie dePaola 125

Chapter 7   More Tomie dePaola Favorites 131

Bibliography 133

Index 137

About the Author 143

♥♥♥ — ♥♥♥ — ♥♥♥ — ♥♥♥ — ♥♥♥ — ♥♥♥

Acknowledgments

I am deeply grateful to those who have supported me in this work from the beginning, many years ago, when some of this work was first self-published. Thanks to Jan Bruton and Lynn Kelly at A Children's Place Bookstore in Portland, Oregon, for first introducing me to Tomie dePaola. It is due to their encouragement that I went to Italy with Tomie in 1983 as part of *il grupo* and was inspired to create meaningful ideas for teachers to use in their classrooms.

Thanks to all of the teachers who have responded so kindly to my work in written and workshop form. I am especially grateful to Phyllis Benke and Jaylin Redden-Hefty, dear friends and teachers who tested and used many of these ideas in their classrooms.

Deep and special thanks to Bob Hechtel, Tomie dePaola's personal assistant, who once again was instrumental in helping me pull all of this work together.

To Sherry Foreman Litwack, editor for my initial work—many thanks to you for your help and support. To my present editor, Suzanne Barchers—your patience has been infinite. Thanks for your unending guidance and support and for your wisdom and kind encouragement. And to Ben, graphic artist extraordinaire—thanks for taking on this project.

Doris and Eric Kimmel, always my best fans, I have no words to describe my thanks for your unending friendship and support. My friends in the Just-Off-Klickitat Book Club—thanks for keeping me reading books other than those for children and for being "my calendar sisters."

For Bill, my true love, *pace e bene*. I love you. You have been and always will be my anchor.

Finally, thank you Tomie, for your belief in my work, for providing the most incredible books to share with children, for your unending support of educators, for being such an inspiration to us all, and especially for showing us how to live and love life!

For all the children and teachers everywhere who love Tomie dePaola's books—*grazie*. Share a favorite Tomie dePaola book with a friend and fall in love with reading all over again.

Introduction

Tomie dePaola

Dear Educators,

This program created by Val Hornburg has my complete endorsement and represents the way I would like to see the books I write and illustrate amplified in the classroom.

With the advent of more and more classrooms embracing literature-based programs as a way of teaching reading and writing, there has been an avalanche of workbooks, how-to volumes, and teaching aids based on the published works of well-loved children's book authors and illustrators.

Many of these books and programs are created by well-meaning educators without the consent or input of the artists and authors being presented. This is not an infringement of the copyright law or illegal publishing. As long as no artwork or text is reproduced without permission, the authors of these books are well within the copyright law. However, because permission by the authors or illustrators is not necessary, these publications may not *represent the feelings or intent of those involved.*

In this case, you can rest assured that I am in full support of the recommendations in these pages. I hope you and your students will further explore my books using Val's encouragement. Above all, don't forget a very important fact: My books are really meant to be ENJOYED!

Tomie dePaola
New Hampshire, 2005

Introduction
Val Hornburg

Tomie dePaola (pronounced Tommy de-POW-la) is one of the most beloved children's authors and illustrators of all time. He has written and illustrated more than 220 children's books, and many of his books are printed in various languages enjoyed the world over. His stories make us laugh out loud and sometimes make us cry. Always, they touch our hearts with love.

I first met Tomie dePaola in 1982 when he came to Portland, Oregon, to be the grand marshal in a city-wide children's author parade and to autograph books at A Children's Place Bookstore, where I worked part time. I was inspired by his energy, by the way he so gracefully interacted with each adult and child, and by his delight in children and anyone in love with children's books. Tomie awakened in me something that I wanted all of my students to have. This personal connection with Tomie dePaola inspired me to make sure that every student I taught was exposed to his books.

Tomie is the little child in so many of his stories and that child speaks so clearly and connects with children (and adults) of all ages. Whether my students giggle about Tomie's antics in the story about his grandfather in *Tom* or cry about his grandfather's stroke in *Now One Foot, Now the Other,* they sense a connection to Tomie, a person who was once a little boy himself. Tomie seems to get in touch with the child in each one of us and gives birth to stories that make us laugh, cry, or be thankful for our own "child within."

It is in the context of these connections that I have been able to bring reading and writing alive for my students. Tomie dePaola has given me quality literature to share with my students and assist them in learning how to read and write about their own experiences. He inspires children to be authors and illustrators and more importantly, to be themselves. He sets the perfect example for all children (actually for all of us!) in his story *The Art Lesson* when he says, "real artists don't copy!"

If I could recommend anything to teachers who pick up this resource book, it would be to go purchase your very own copy of Tomie de Paola's *The Art Lesson*. I would encourage you to read it and keep it close at hand. By reading the story, you will clearly understand why you won't find patterns for children to cut, copy, or color in this resource book. My goal is to be child-centered—to provide a variety of activities that encourage children to think for *themselves,* to discuss what is meaningful to *them,* to write their *own* stories, and to create their *own* artistic responses.

Literacy is about making connections. In this resource book, you will find literary guides for each Tomie dePaola book included in this work. Each literary guide provides literature-based reading and writing activities that I hope will be springboards for your own ideas and those of your students. I've tried to include activities that integrate the curriculum and develop and deepen the experience of a reading/writing community of learners in the classroom. I believe that together my students and I form a community of learners—and I learn just as much as they do throughout the year.

You will also find that all the activities relate in some way to the Standards for the English Language Arts, co-published by the National Council of Teachers of English and the International Reading Association. For a complete listing of these standards, please consult the *Standards of the English Language Arts,* published in 1996, or the International Reading Association's Web site at www.reading.org.

Some of this work was first self-published and copyrighted in 1993 and 1997. If you purchased my self-published works previously, you will find some of the work familiar, but many of the literary guides in this book are completely new or expanded. I hope you will find them helpful in preparing your classroom curriculum.

Biographical Information about Tomie dePaola

Tomie dePaola (pronounced Tommy de-POW-la) was born on September 15, 1934, to Joseph and Florence (Downey) dePaola in Meriden, Connecticut. He is of Irish and Italian descent. He has two sisters, Maureen and Judie. He had one brother, Joseph.

When he was a little boy, Tomie used to take a book, a flashlight, and a special pencil that his grandfather had given him, crawl beneath the white sheets down to the foot of his bed, and draw pictures. It was his secret place . . . until his mother changed the sheets!

Tomie took art classes in high school. After he graduated, he went to art school, where he says he "spent four years learning to draw everything—tin cans, dogs, cats, horses, people, trees—and I practiced and practiced and practiced."

Each book takes Tomie a different amount of time to write. "Some stories take only a few days or weeks," he says, "but some take years." The illustrations usually take him a few months to complete. Tomie has illustrated more than 200 books and he has written the stories for more than half of those books. The first book he illustrated was *Sound,* by Lisa Miller, in 1965. The first book he both wrote and illustrated was *The Wonderful Dragon of Timlin,* in 1966.

Tomie dePaola has received many awards, including the Caldecott Honor Award from the American Library Association (ALA) for *Strega Nona,* and the Newbery Honor Award from ALA for *26 Fairmount Avenue,* the first in a book series about Tomie's childhood.

Today Tomie dePaola lives in the town of New London, New Hampshire. He is not married and has no children. He has an Airedale puppy named Brontë. Tomie's new studio is attached to a 200-year-old barn. His house is only a few feet from the barn. Both are set on the edge of a large meadow full of wonderful flower gardens. There is also a wonderful swimming pool that Tomie uses to entertain his many friends. He also has an ice cream machine and a large popcorn machine on wheels. Of course, his favorite snack is popcorn!

Tomie loves to cook, read, and watch movies. His favorite color is white and Christmas is his favorite holiday. Every Christmas, his house and barn are decorated with candles, flowers, and Christmas trees. One year he had ten Christmas trees! Tomie also loves his birthday. In 2004 Tomie celebrated his seventieth birthday. He threw a party for 160 of his special friends. What a celebration it was!

Tomie loves to keep busy. A newspaper writer once wrote that Tomie dePaola is "a combination of Elton John and the Energizer bunny, a talented man who never seems to run out of steam." It's so true.

For more biographical information about Tomie dePaola, see Chapter 5, *A Visit with Tomie dePaola: A Video Resource Guide* and *Tomie dePaola: His Art & His Stories,* by Barbara Elleman. This is a beautifully written, comprehensive look at Tomie dePaola, a most useful resource that provides an in-depth look into the world of this beloved children's author and illustrator. You can also check out www.Tomie.com, the official Tomie dePaola Web site. On the site you will find up-to-date information on Tomie—his travel schedule for author signings and appearances, information about his latest books, and musings about his life today as well as his childhood.

How to Use the Literary Guides

It is my hope that these literary guides will be exactly that—guides for you to use as you prepare to share some of Tomie dePaola's books in the classroom. Whether you decide to focus on an in-depth Tomie dePaola unit for several weeks or weave Tomie dePaola's books throughout your existing integrated units of study, I hope the ideas and activities presented in this book will assist you in reading Tomie dePaola's books with your students. Enjoy!

Each literary guide includes the following elements to assist you:

SUMMARY

These are more in-depth summaries than many other guides provide, as I know teachers often want a little bit more information about the stories they are to share before reading them in the classroom. With the autobiographical books especially, I have tried to include important background information about Tomie dePaola in relation to the books he has written.

PRE-READING ACTIVITIES

At least one pre-reading activity is provided for each story. These are to assist you in engaging children in the reading process so that they are thinking about their own lives as they hear many of the stories. It's all about making connections!

MAKING PREDICTIONS

This section assists you in specifically talking about each book—looking at the covers of the book and helping children create connections to the text they are about to experience.

READING THE STORY

In this section, specific ways to maximize the experience of reading the text are provided. In some instances, ideas include particular places to stop reading the story purely for enjoyment or to make further predictions. There may be suggestions about how to reread a book after the initial reading—how to revisit it for additional understanding. This is also the reason I have including the following section in each literary guide.

THINKING CRITICALLY ABOUT THE TEXT

Through literature discussions children make meaningful connections to stories and increase their understanding and comprehension of them. The questions listed in this section are designed to assist you in your literature discussion of each Tomie dePaola book. You and your students may have additional questions of your own.

SHARING PERSONAL EXPERIENCES

Because many Tomie dePaola stories evoke personal memories in children, it is important to allow time to talk about these experiences in the classroom. In sharing our personal stories with one another, we continue to further our own comprehension of them and build an even closer learning community.

RESPONDING TO THE TEXT

There are many ways for children to respond to the texts you read. In this section of each literary guide, several meaningful options are presented for you and your students to choose from. It is my hope that some of these ideas will bring Tomie dePaola's stories even more alive for your children. In each literary guide, you will find ideas for writing, art, and integrated language arts. In addition, some books lend themselves to response activities in drama, science, social studies, or math. In these instances, additional responses activities are provided.

Chapter 1

The Autobiographical Stories

INTRODUCTION

Some of the most popular and endearing books that Tomie dePaola has written are those written about his own childhood. Simply put, children and adults alike can relate to the little boy Tomie in the stories he shares about spending time with his grandparents, with his family, and at school. I know you will enjoy reading these books with your students.

In this chapter, I focus on the autobiographical picture books Tomie dePaola has written and illustrated. You will find more fine stories about Tomie dePaola's childhood in his award-winning *26 Fairmount Avenue* series. I encourage you to introduce your students to these, too.

I present the autobiographical stories in the order I share them in the classroom rather than in the order they were written. Many titles lend themselves beautifully to fostering community building in the classroom. Read the summaries of the books included in this chapter and choose the Tomie dePaola title with which you want to begin.

Andy, That's My Name

SUMMARY

This story was written and illustrated by Tomie dePaola in 1973. It is the story of a young boy named Andy and the importance of names. Andy takes his name around wherever he goes and when he runs into some older kids, he hopes to join in on their play. Instead, the kids take Andy's name away from him and begin playing around with his name on their own. Andy becomes very frustrated and gathers up all of the letters. As he takes them away, he says, "I may be little, but I'm very important!"

In *Andy, That's My Name* we see an autobiographical connection to Tomie dePaola because Tomie didn't always spell his name as it appears now, although it is the correct spelling. The teachers Tomie dePaola had when he was younger wouldn't hear of him having an unconventional spelling for his name, so until Tomie was in high school, his name was spelled T-o-m-m-y. Can you and your students see why Tomie has such powerful feelings about names?

Although the story of *Andy, That's My Name* can be shared at any time with your children, I've shared it successfully each year as the school year begins. During the first days of school it is important to establish a child's sense of belonging to the class and especially to the classroom that becomes home away from home for nine months of the year. What better way to do this than to stress each child's importance by honoring their names and perhaps displaying them around the classroom. It also helps the children learn each other's names at the beginning of the school year.

PRE-READING ACTIVITIES

As a whole class, discuss the importance of each person's name. Ask questions such as:

- Who named you?
- Why did your parents pick your name?
- Were you named after someone?
- Did your parents pick your name because they liked the sound of it?

Encourage children to share their responses with the whole group. If some children do not know why their parents selected their names, give them the chance to talk with their parents that evening and to share their new knowledge with the class the next day.

MAKING PREDICTIONS

Have children look at the front and back cover of the book and predict what they think the story will be about:

- Why do you think the title is *Andy, That's My Name*?
- What do you notice about Andy?
- After looking at the back cover, where letters of the alphabet are all jumbled together, do you have any other predictions about the story?

READING THE STORY

Read *Andy, That's My Name* to the class slowly, allowing time for children to see what is happening in each of the pictures. As the big kids in the story start playing with Andy's name, children may naturally chime in with the new words being formed. It is helpful to use your finger and follow underneath the words as children chime in.

THINKING CRITICALLY ABOUT THE TEXT

- What are some ways the kids in the story change Andy's name?
- How can you tell that Andy is bothered by the other kids playing with his name?
- What clues does Tomie dePaola, as the author, reveal through the text?
- What clues does Tomie dePaola, as the illustrator, give us through the pictures?
- Why do you think all the characters are in costume?

SHARING PERSONAL EXPERIENCES

- Have you ever had an experience like Andy where older kids didn't let you play their games? Where were you and what happened?

RESPONDING TO THE TEXT: INTEGRATED LANGUAGE ARTS

Name Rhymes

Children write their names on a piece of paper and work with a partner to list any words that rhyme with their names. If no real words rhyme with a child's name, encourage partners to think up silly nonsense words that rhyme with the name. For example: VAL—pal, Al, gal, and so forth.

With younger children, use some of their names to demonstrate each name games strategy more slowly. Each day for a week you might take a different child's name and have the whole class think of words that rhyme with that name. While children are brainstorming possibilities, record these on a list under the child's name. Post this list where all children can see it and add to it any rhyming words they think of later. As children catch on, they can write their own names and rhyming words on paper and post them around the room.

Name Game Challenges

After children catch on to the rhyming name game, present other name game strategies to the whole class (or to the children who are ready). These games are a lot of fun. Children (and adults) never seem to tire of playing with their names. Of course, there are many other name games you can do—here are just a few.

Adding on

Children think of any letters they can add to their names to make new words. For example: VAL—valentine, oval, and so forth.

Hidden words

Children write out their whole names (first and last) and try to see how many words they can create using all of the letters. For example: VAL HORNBURG—horn, burn, run, bug, rug, hub, bag, van, or, born, ran, bun . . .

Name songs

Write a rhyming song as a class using children's names and their rhyming words. The names of your children can be integrated into a song to the tune of "B-I-N-G-O" or to jump rope rhymes. This song, incorporating all class names, could become a class theme song to begin your day, to share with visitors or parents, or to use whenever you sing with your class.

RESPONDING TO THE TEXT: WRITING

How I Was Named

Children write or dictate how they got their names. Put their writing on display in the classroom at eye level so that all children can read each other's work.

Class Books

Make a class book (pop-up, accordion, bound, etc.) with each page representing a child. Pages can have pictures or pop-ups of each child and a little explanation of how they were named. Children and parents love looking at this type of book all year long.

Poetry

Children make an acrostic poem using their name. First, have them write the letters in their names down the left hand side of the page. After each letter, have them write words or phrases that describe themselves (what they look like, their interests, their personalities, etc.). These poems look wonderful when displayed in the classroom. *Note:* younger children can do this with a group or with an older-grade buddy.

EXAMPLE:

B elieves in FUN!

I nterested in everything

L oves pasta

L ives in Portland

RESPONDING TO THE TEXT: ART

Name Painting

For many years, I have done the following art project during the first weeks of school with my children. I encourage students to create large, artistic versions of their names that remain displayed on our classroom walls throughout the school year. This visual display gives everyone who walks into the classroom an important message about those who work and learn in our classroom. I want people to have the feeling that it is "our" classroom, not "my" classroom. Not only is the environment enhanced by the brightness of each child's name (as well as mine), but it also helps establish ownership in the classroom. Children know that we all must take responsibility for our learning as well as our learning environment.

Have each child create his or her name artistically in some way to display around the classroom. Children can draw and paint or color their names using bright colors and designs. With older children (second grade and above) I have taught them how to draw and paint their names using block or "bubble" letters. I give my students 18" × 24" white construction paper because I have large, open spaces above my bulletin boards in my classroom, but any paper 8 ½" × 11" or larger will suffice.

Younger children can write their name on a piece of construction paper, outline it with black pen or paint, and then create lovely designs around their names. In kindergarten, some children begin school not knowing how to write their names. I either write everyone's name on a piece of paper with pencil and then have children paint over their name with black paint or large markers, or I wait until

SAM   SAM

January when everyone is able to write his or her name and then complete the above steps in the art process.

After the names are completed, we meet as a group and put the names in alphabetical order according to *first* names. (We are so often put into ABC order according to our last names!) This is a nice way to introduce alphabetical order or to learn to say the alphabet. Don't forget to add your own name! As soon as possible, display the names around the room high on the walls or wherever space permits.

Steps in the name painting activity

1. Children draw their name on a piece of paper the appropriate size for display in your classroom. Older children may want to use block letters.
2. Names are painted or colored using brightly colored paints, crayons, markers, and so on.
3. The whole class gathers to put the names in ABC order or in another order agreed upon by the group.
4. The teacher displays the names around the classroom.
5. At the end of the year, names are taken down, glued onto brightly colored butcher paper, and used to create autograph posters signed by class members. On the last day of school, the children and teacher(s) sign autographs or just their signature around each person's name, thus making an autograph poster—a delightful reminder of the school year.

A few notes

As new children join the class during the school year, have them create a name painting or drawing and put it up next to the last name already posted on the wall. If a child leaves in the middle of the school year, take down the person's name and go through the autographing process to create an autographed going-away gift.

One more idea

The same type of art response can be used to create a permanent bulletin board display of children's work. Instead of using large construction paper, use file folders. Children create their name designs on one side or end of the file folder and leave the neighboring side or opposite end empty for ongoing pieces of their writing and artwork.

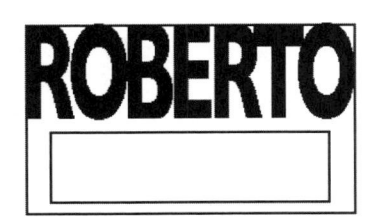

ANN   ROBERTO

Oliver Button Is a Sissy

SUMMARY

In this book, Oliver is a boy who is called a sissy because he likes to do different things. He likes to sing, dance, dress up, and pretend he is a movie star. He does not like to do the things that "boys are supposed to do." Oliver loves to dance, so his mom enrolls him in dancing school where Oliver excells. Even though the teasing continues, Oliver practices and practices his dancing to prepare for a big talent show. Oliver does not win the talent show, but everyone around him recognizes that he indeed has talent and that perhaps it's alright to like different things.

This story is autobiographical in that Tomie dePaola himself loved to read and draw and took tap dancing lessons. He became an accomplished tap dancer and competed in talent shows and competitions. He won some competitions and still loves to dance today.

PRE-READING ACTIVITIES: A PRE-READING QUESTIONNAIRE

Create and distribute a questionnaire for your students to fill out that looks something like this:

Things girls like to do:	Things boys like to do:

Give children several minutes to list a few ideas on the chart you have given them. Then, elicit some of their responses to write on a similar chart you have created on the board.

Ask children if they have listed activities that are specific to boys or girls. Why or why not? Follow up with a discussion on what it might mean to call someone a sissy. How would that feel? What other names do children use intentionally to make fun of someone else or to hurt someone's feelings? Encourage children to share any that are appropriate. This makes an excellent topic for a class meeting.

MAKING PREDICTIONS

Show the front cover of the book to the children and discuss:

- Why do you think the book is called *Oliver Button Is a Sissy*?
- Are all people who paint sissies?

Look at the back cover of the story.

- Do you have any other predictions about the story?

READING THE STORY

Read *Oliver Button Is a Sissy* to your class slowly, allowing them to think about many of the situations in the text that they may have also experienced in their young lives.

THINKING CRITICALLY ABOUT THE TEXT

- What are some of the things Oliver likes to do?
- Why is Oliver called a sissy?
- Can you tell how Oliver feels when he has been called a sissy or has been teased by schoolmates?
- How do you think Oliver feels to be chosen last when teams are divided up?
- Oliver practices and practices for the talent show but doesn't win. How does he react? How do his parents and Miss Leah react? His classmates?

SHARING PERSONAL EXPERIENCES

- Have you ever been teased before or called hurtful names?
- Have you ever been chosen last in a game or felt that you had been chosen last? How did that feel?
- What is something that you don't mind practicing over and over again? Why is practice important?
- Have you ever been a star at something?

RESPONDING TO THE TEXT: ART

Starring!

Help all of your students know and believe that they are stars! Encourage students to think about and draw or paint a picture of themselves doing something they love to do. It might be riding a bike, playing soccer, painting, sketching, or playing a musical instrument. Give each child a piece of paper with instructions to fill the paper with a color drawing that shows something that they just love to do. After the artwork is created, display it on a bulletin board entitled, "Starring," "Our 2nd-grade Stars!" or something similar. You might even run a strand or two of white lights around the outside edge of the bulletin board for special effects. The goal is for all children to know that they are loved and appreciated no matter what their interests, no matter what their talents.

To make the bulletin board project even simpler, children could bring in a photo of themselves doing some activity or sport or you could take photos of them at school dramatizing an activity. These photos could be put up by themselves, put next to the illustration each child has drawn or painted (see above), or put onto star-shaped pieces of poster board and posted outside your classroom door. All those who walk through the door will know that they are entering a room full of stars!

These Are a Few of My Favorite Things . . . to Do!

Some children may not want to draw themselves doing only one sport or activity. You could give your students paper that is divided equally into fourths and encourage them to illustrate four different activities that they like to do. These could be put on the bulletin board described above or put together into a classroom book for your shared book collection. Be sure to create a page or illustration for yourself!

RESPONDING TO THE TEXT: WRITING

Creating and Signing a Pledge

During a classroom meeting or discussion, discuss the concept of a *pledge* with your children. Use a dictionary to look up the actual definition if needed. Discuss with your children some of the following:

- After reading *Oliver Button Is a Sissy,* how might we pledge to be with each other in our classroom, on the playground, everywhere?
- How do you like to be treated?

Create a simple pledge that children craft, decorate, and sign to be posted in the classroom. An example might be: The members of this classroom will not tease or call people names. Post the pledge in a prominent area of the classroom so that all who enter can see it. You will find more ideas on classroom meetings and creating pledges with your children in the books *Teaching Children to Care,* by Ruth Charney, *Ways We Want Our Class to Be,* by the Child Development Project, and *Because We Can Change the World,* by Mara Sapon-Shevin.

RESPONDING TO THE TEXT: DRAMA

A Talent Show!

Host your very own classroom talent show! Ask children to think about talents they have and encourage them to share them with each other in an informal talent show. For those children who don't feel particularly talented, encourage them to memorize a short song or poem, or to think about a special talent they may have in caring for a younger brother or sister, helping mom and dad with something at home, or being a special friend to someone. Everyone has talents and gifts—sometimes we just don't know what they are!

The Art Lesson

SUMMARY

This is an autobiographical look into the early art experiences of Tomie dePaola. Tommy knows very early in life that he wants to be an artist when he grows up, and with the help of his cousins (who are artists) and a very supportive family, Tommy creates his artwork all the time.

Tommy arrives in first grade ready to set his artistic creativity loose! He comes prepared with his brand new box of sixty-four Crayola crayons to learn new techniques in art and to express himself. But soon he learns that the art teacher, Mrs. Bowers, comes once every other week and only gives out *one* piece of paper. Imagine Tommy's dismay during art class when the teacher tells the children to watch carefully and copy her. ("Real artists don't copy!" is Tommy's immediate reply!) And the teachers won't let him use his own set of crayons because his are different from the rest of the class.

The ending is a happy one, of course, and a message to teachers about the importance in letting all children express their own individuality and creativity.

PRE-READING ACTIVITIES

Gather your children together and discuss:

- Do you remember what you thought about before you began your first day of kindergarten? Were you nervous? Were you afraid to leave your mom?
- What did you think school would be like?
- What did you hope to learn in school?

Older children can fill out an anticipation guide (see below), activating their early school experiences. After filling these out, children can share their answers with others before reading the story. The anticipation guide may be most appropriate for second graders or older; you can ask younger children the questions orally.

MAKING PREDICTIONS

Read the story to your children and discuss:

- What do you notice about the cover?
- Where do you think the story takes place?
- Who do you think is on the cover?
- What kind of art lesson do you think it might be?

Note: You may want to read the dedication to assist children in making more specific predictions. You could also return to it after the first reading of the book.

READING THE STORY

Read *The Art Lesson* to your class. Children quickly discover that this story is an *autobiographical story* about Tomie dePaola, although they may not yet use that term.

THINKING CRITICALLY ABOUT THE TEXT

- What are some new things you learned about Tomie dePaola's life by reading *The Art Lesson*?
- What is the main setting of the story?
- Why do you think Tommy brings his set of crayons back to school even though his teacher told him to leave them at home?
- What do you think about Miss Landers, Tommy's first-grade teacher?
- Is Mrs. Bowers different in her approach to Tommy (and other children) than Miss Landers? If so, how?

Anticipation Guide
The Art Lesson

Name _____

STRONGLY AGREE **STRONGLY DISAGREE**

1. I was excited about going to school when I began kindergarten.

   ☺ _____ ☹

2. There were certain things I wanted to learn at school.

   ☺ _____ ☹

3. My parents let me draw as much as I wanted when I was young.

   ☺ _____ ☹

4. My first teachers let me draw whenever I wanted.

   ☺ _____ ☹

5. I remember some art accidents or had a hard time with art during my first years of school.

   ☺ _____ ☹

6. Art is one of my favorite things to do at school.

   ☺ _____ ☹

7. I have the chance to do some artwork every day.

   ☺ _____ ☹

SHARING PERSONAL EXPERIENCES

- Does Tomie dePaola's story remind you of any experiences you've had? What are they?

RESPONDING TO THE TEXT: INTEGRATED LANGUAGE ARTS

Interviews

Children interview their peers and/or parents about their favorite color and create a simple bar graph of the results. The results can then be shared with all who were involved.

Alphabetizing

Using a box of crayons, children alphabetize the crayons according to color name. Partners can work together to check each other's ABC order. As a challenge, a group of two to four children can alphabetize an entire box of sixty-four crayons. This is great practice for both alphabetizing and reading the names of colors!

Create a Color!

Children pretend that their job is to name new crayons! Binney & Smith, which makes Crayola brand crayons, actually sponsors such contests, enlisting help from the public in naming new colors. As a crayon developer, children can create a new color name for a crayon based on the colors that they like to use in their drawings. Then, they can write an ad or create a commercial that advertises their new crayon color.

Have a "New Crayon Color" election

Have a contest in your classroom. As part of the election, interested children make short speeches convincing others why their color is necessary for outstanding student artwork. Encourage children to include examples of the color and artwork that uses it. The winning color can be used to create a new bulletin board or mural for the classroom, designed by children.

Pantomime

Children pantomime their favorite things to do and have their classmates guess what those activities or hobbies are. This game can be played like charades, with children forming teams or small groups.

Reader's Theatre

Children can do an informal reader's theatre performance of *The Art Lesson,* with several students narrating the story. The speaking parts can be read by children playing the parts of:

Tommy	Tomie's Dad
Tomie's mom	Jeannie
Joe	Miss Landers
Miss Bird	Mrs. Bowers

The CRAYON CREATOR

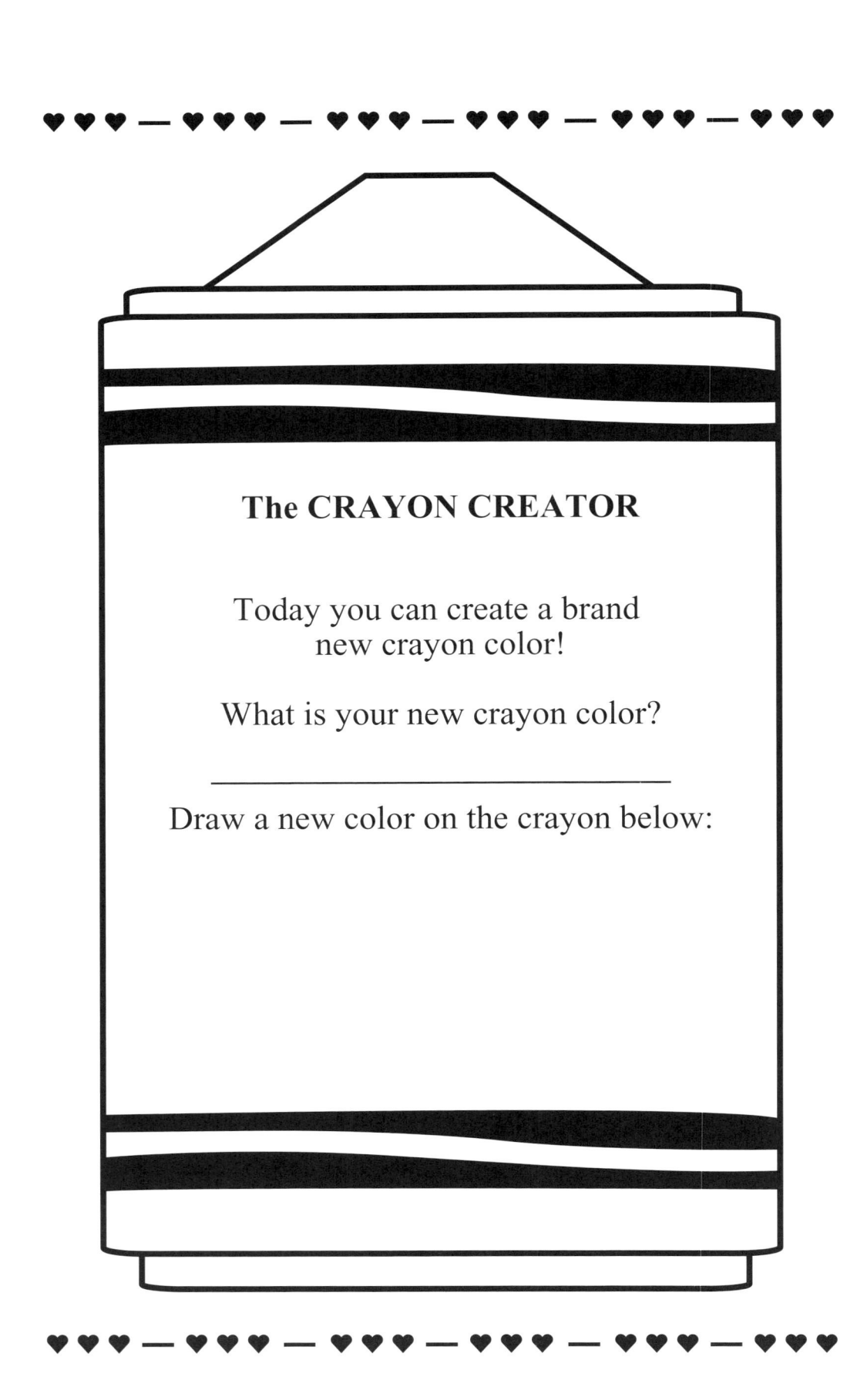

Today you can create a brand new crayon color!

What is your new crayon color?
_____

Draw a new color on the crayon below:

Children holding parts can read them during the narration as their speaking part occurs. Children could also make props or wear costumes. The fun and learning occur through the reading of the story line, attending to the punctuation, inflection of voices, and children getting ready to read their parts.

Another option is for remaining children to pantomime or act out the story while the reading is done. The more children you can involve, the better!

RESPONDING TO THE TEXT: WRITING

Character Descriptions

What words would you use to describe Tommy as a child? Write a brief character description as if you are another student in his class or a friend from the neighborhood.

Your Favorites

Tomie dePaola used to draw and draw all of the time. Write about your favorite things to do. Write all about your special interests and any interesting stories surrounding them.

Disasters

In kindergarten Tomie dePaola had the experience of paint cracking and blowing off of his artwork on a blustery day. This had to be both frustrating and disappointing. Have you had any artistic "disasters" happen to you? If so, what happened? Or perhaps some kinds of art or art techniques frustrate you. What are they? Have you learned a way to keep yourself from getting frustrated in the future?

Getting Your Own Crayons

A lot of adults probably remember getting or using their very first box of Crayola crayons. Do you remember when you got your first box of crayons and how you felt? What did you draw first? Did you have to protect your crayons from others (like siblings)? Write about your experiences.

RESPONDING TO THE TEXT: ART

Your Favorite Art Lesson

What kind of art do you love to do? Share that love by teaching your students your favorite art technique. Talk about how you discovered the art process or technique, share examples of what you and others have done with it, and provide time for children to experiment with the technique on their own. After children have experimented with the new art project or process, ask them if they enjoyed it and to explain why or why not.

Sharing Art Ideas

Ask children to share their favorite art projects. Encourage them to bring in previously done projects that they enjoyed making. Have children discuss the art techniques or lessons they learned from their art projects.

Art Display

Ask children if their parents and teacher display their artwork. If they do, where do they display it? Have children draw or sketch a picture showing where their artwork is displayed, as Tomie dePaola did in *The Art Lesson*. Revisit the book to find that his art was displayed in his bedroom, on the walls of his home, in his Dad's barber shop, and other places.

If art isn't your love, do your parents or teachers display something else you have done (e.g., writing, sports ribbons, trophies, certificates) in a special way? Perhaps you are a collector instead. Where and how do you display your treasures?

Self-Portraits

There are several self-portraits of Tomie dePaola in *The Art Lesson*. Have children begin a file of self-portraits for the year by drawing, painting, or sketching themselves doing something they love to do. Provide opportunities for your students to create more than one self-portrait during the year and have them date their artwork and place each in a portfolio. Be sure to use a variety of art mediums when doing self-portraits. Choose *your* favorite way to draw or create a self-portrait first when sharing art strategies or techniques with children. It will most likely be their favorite self-portrait of the year because the art medium you are teaching them is your favorite! We teach best what we love!

Design a Crayon-Art Activity Book

Encourage children to brainstorm a list of all of the art activities they think of that use crayons. Have them list these on a chart and sign up to illustrate a page for a classroom crayon-art activity book. Children can name the activity, describe how to do it and list the steps involved, and include a miniature example on the page. It can become a classroom reference book for children to use when they have free time or need a new art idea.

Note: You may want to have some art reference books available for children to browse through if they run out of ideas. These will spark their creativity and encourage them to come up with additional ideas of their own.

Now One Foot, Now the Other

SUMMARY

Now One Foot, Now the Other is the story of an endearing relationship between a little boy named Bobby and his grandfather, Bob. Bobby, named after his grandfather, learns how to walk with Bob's assistance. They share a special activity, building blocks, that brings both of them great enjoyment. When Bob has a stroke, Bobby is heartbroken. He and his parents don't know if Bob will recover. Through love, faith, and determination Bobby helps his grandfather walk again, "now one foot, now the other . . ."

This story is an autobiographical glimpse into special times shared between Tomie dePaola and his grandfather, Tom. It is a powerful story to use with children and it launches tender discussions regarding important adults in their lives—those who bring them special joy or ones who have suffered a similar medical experience. Due to the nature of this story, be ready for follow-up discussions regarding strokes and illnesses that can affect people who are older than we are.

This story can be used at the beginning of the year in observance of Grandparent's Day or any time during the year. It continues the theme of friendship and sharing. Most of us have special adults who shared precious moments with us during our childhood.

PRE-READING ACTIVITIES

Have a discussion using the questions below to facilitate children's thinking about their experiences with grandparents and/or special people in their lives.

- Are your grandparents living?
- If they are, do you get to see them often? If so, how often?
- If they are no longer living, do you remember spending time with them or do you have other adults or family members that you spend a lot of time with? If so, who and what do you remember?
- Do you have special memories of times you've shared with these people? What made the times memorable?

MAKING PREDICTIONS

Show the cover of the book to your students and discuss:

- Can you predict what the story will be about?
- Who do you think is on the cover?
- What do you think Tomie dePaola means by the title *Now One Foot, Now the Other*?

READING THE STORY

Many adults cry when they read this beautiful story for the first time. Be sure to read it and enjoy it yourself first before sharing it with your students. When you read the story with your children, take time to look at the pictures, especially the building blocks with pictures and letters on them. (Tomie dePaola still has this special set of blocks, although now they grace his living room. He often uses the blocks to spell out special messages to his guests!)

As you read the part of the story where Bobby learns about Bob's stroke, observe children's faces to see how they are reacting. Sometimes this story evokes memories of difficult experiences children have had. It is important to be aware of how stories trigger memories.

Children really relate to *Now One Foot, Now the Other* because "Bobby knows best" in the story, believing that he can make a difference in Bob's recovery—and he does!

THINKING CRITICALLY ABOUT THE TEXT

- What is special about the relationship between Bob and Bobby?
- What word would you use to describe Bob?
- How does Tomie dePaola show what Bobby and the others are feeling? How can you tell when Bobby is feeling happy, lonely, or upset? Are there any clues other than facial expressions?
- Tomie dePaola uses only a few colors to illustrate *Now One Foot, Now the Other.* How is this different from other stories he has illustrated?

SHARING PERSONAL EXPERIENCES

- Do you have special memories about someone teaching you how to walk, read, ride a bike, or fish? Perhaps it was something else you learned how to do. Where were you, what did you learn, and who was helping you?

Encourage children to go home and discuss with their parents the memories of grandparents or special adults who come to mind. Discussion with parents may help children remember and visualize the experiences or pieces of those experiences they have forgotten.

RESPONDING TO THE TEXT: WRITING

Diary Entries

Children can write entries from Bobby's point of view for the days when he and Bob spent Bobby's fifth birthday together, when he first heard about Bob's having a stroke, when Bob came home from the hospital, when Bob made a "sneeze" sound when Bobby built blocks and the elephant block tumbled, or when Bobby taught Bob how to walk again. If children work together in small groups to write these diary entries, the entries can later be assembled into a classroom book for sharing.

Life Changes

Have children write about how they think Bobby might change as a result of his experiences with his grandfather's illness.

Using Your Senses

To prepare for this writing response, have children think about a special memory—a time spent with a grandparent or special adult. Have them close their eyes and try to actually relive that memory in their mind. Ask some of the following questions:

- What do you see?
- Do you recall any special smells in the air or room you are in?
- What about things you touch? Is there a texture to those things?
- Do you hear any specific sounds as you relive the memory?
- Finally, did you taste anything, like the hot dogs and ice cream Bob and Bobby shared on Bobby's fifth birthday? What tastes do you remember?

Note: This activity may evoke painful memories in some children. If a child seems upset, you may want to give the child an opportunity to speak privately with you or a school counselor.

Stories

Have students write (or draw a picture and dictate a story) about a time they shared with a grandparent or special person. Encourage them to capture the memory descriptively. Have them visualize the experience through their five senses (see above). Then, add any other descriptive adjectives they think about in terms of that special person. Is that person gentle, caring, patient, funny? If children are drawing and dictating the story, encourage each child to draw descriptively, using as many details as possible.

Making a book

After children write about or draw their special memory, they might want to make a book to put their writing in. There are many types of books, including hand-bound books, pop-ups, and tall books. The more ways children know how to "publish" their writing, the more they seem to write!

Thank you letters

If children publish (edit, revise, and bind) their stories, they can send them (or a copy) to their special person as a way to say thank you. The story can be sent off immediately with a little note or saved for Grandparent's Day (if their special person is a grandparent) or another holiday. Children can do this activity even if their special person has passed away; they can share their stories with someone else they care about.

There are two sides to every story (point of view)

Once children have written their version of a special memory, you could encourage them to invite the special person (if possible) to write his or her version of the experience. What do they remember about the child and the day of the event? These stories could be placed side by side in a book to be treasured for years to come. If any pictures were taken, include them too! As an optional idea, stories could be audiotaped or videotaped as well.

An Old Saying

There is an old saying about "putting your foot in your mouth." What does that mean? Find out and then share or write about experiences when you have "put your foot in your mouth." These could be written anonymously and posted. Then children could have fun guessing who had each experience.

RESPONDING TO THE TEXT: ART

Time Capsules

Thinking about the year to come, discuss with your children:

- What are some of your goals for the coming year?
- Would you like to become better at reading, writing, art, math, or other skills (perhaps even making friends) during this school year?
- What will you need to do in order to meet your goal(s)? How can I help you?

Children can draw, sketch, and/or write about their goals and put them in miniature time capsules. Decorated and rolled-up paper tubes work well.

Close to the year's end, have children open up the time capsules and reflect:

- Did you meet some of your goals or learn some of the things you had hoped you would?
- Who helped you? Other children? Teachers? Your parents?

**Draw a roll with
ties on end**

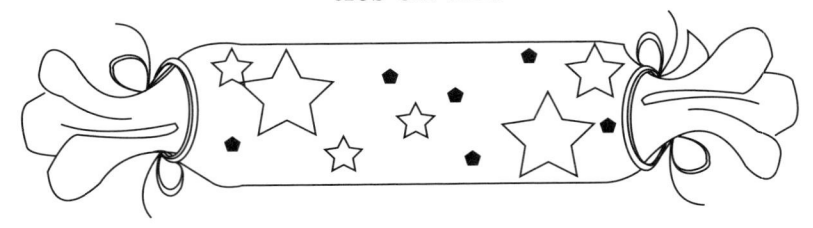

Making Friendship Blocks

Using the block pattern in this literary guide (enlarged and copied onto vellum), children construct and decorate a block that represents them. They can include:

- their name or a design that represents them (initials are fine).
- their grade (or possibly a class symbol).
- their favorites—like animals, stories, songs, places (symbols or words).
- other designs they think of.

Put these on display somewhere prominent in the classroom. They are fun to look at and children learn about their classmates by noting their "favorites" depicted on the sides of the student blocks.

Just like Tomie dePaola . . .

You might have children make extra blocks with letters of the alphabet on them. Then, just like Tomie dePaola, you could use them to spell out simple messages to the people who visit you in the classroom.

Create Your Own Footwear

The possibilities are endless if students decide to do some research, especially in the area of sports footwear. Commercials abound in this area and children can design their own shoes tailored to their tastes and lifestyles. It might be fun to send some of these designs off to the shoe companies!

RESPONDING TO THE TEXT: MATH

Bare Feet

Children get giggly over this, but what fun to have each child trace one foot (without a shoe and sock on) onto construction or graph paper and . . .

- determine and compare the length of his or her foot (size) to other feet in the class.
- determine and compare the perimeters of feet in the class.
- determine the area of his or her foot in centimeters (trace foot onto centimeter graph paper).
- have children try to find something else in the classroom that is the same area as their foot (a challenge).
- convert the size of the foot in inches to centimeters.

Comparisons can be recorded on classroom graphs using a traced foot of each child.

Now One Foot, Now the Other
Block Design Activity

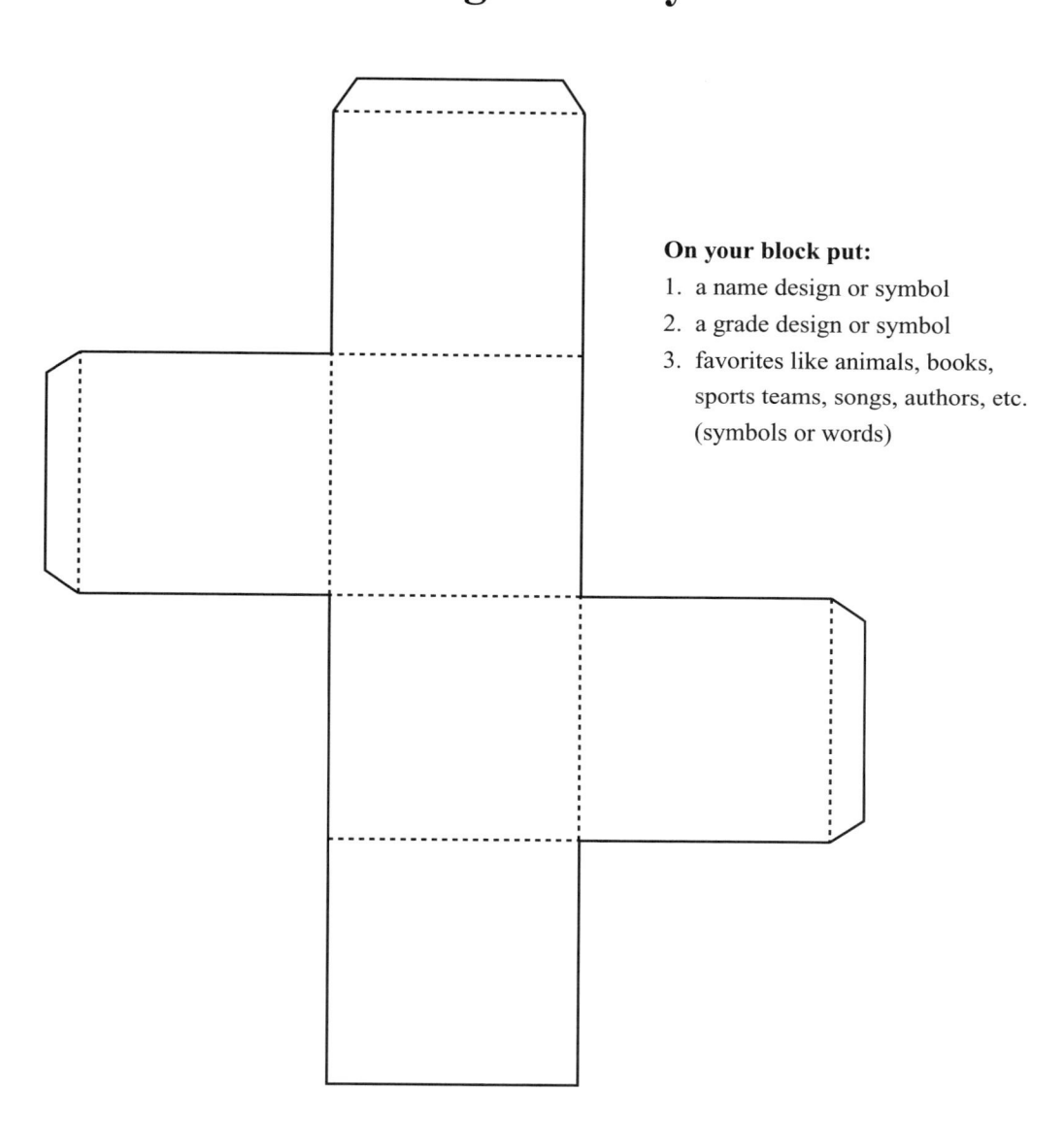

On your block put:
1. a name design or symbol
2. a grade design or symbol
3. favorites like animals, books, sports teams, songs, authors, etc. (symbols or words)

RESPONDING TO THE TEXT: COOKING OR PRINTING

There are plastic footprint cookie cutters available at cooking stores that can be used if you bake with children. The cookie cutters can also be used to make printed book covers by dipping cutters into paint and stamping them on paper or creating a foot-shaped stamp with a sponge.

Tom

SUMMARY

Tom is another story about the special relationship of Tomie dePaola and his Irish grandfather Tom. Tom and Tommy, we have learned, are the best of friends. Tom shares lots of stories with Tommy. When Tom teaches Tommy how to do a trick using chicken feet, Tommy decides to try the trick out on his friends at school. Somehow the trick isn't as funny when it's being played on them. Tommy gets in trouble and is never to bring chicken feet to school ever again.

This story is great to use in conjunction with reading *Now One Foot, Now the Other*, another story about Tomie dePaola and his grandfather.

PRE-READING ACTIVITIES

If you and your children have already listened to *Now One Foot, Now the Other*, create a list of words that describe Tomie's grandfather (Bob in the story). If not, brainstorm a list of words that describe your idea of what an "ideal" grandfather is like.

MAKING PREDICTIONS

Show the front cover of the book to your children and discuss:

- What do you notice about Tom on the front cover—about his clothing, about what he might be like?
- What words would you use to describe the place where Tom is standing?

Show the back cover of the story and discuss:

- What do you notice about Tom and Tommy in the picture?
- When could the picture have been taken?
- Why do you think Tomie dePaola painted the picture using only a few colors?
- How is the back cover different from the front cover?
- Have you ever seen pictures or photos like the one on the back cover before?

READING THE STORY: SETTING THE STAGE— A SENSORY EXPERIENCE

- Have you ever been to a butcher's shop before? Or to the butcher section of a grocery store? What was it like?

Ask children who have been to a butcher shop (or section of a grocery store) to help those who have never had this experience. Encourage them to close their eyes and use their senses to describe what a friend might experience if he or she walked into a butcher shop. Ask:

- What might you smell?
- What are some of the items you might see?
- What would you hear?
- Would you be able to taste or touch anything at the butcher shop?

Encourage children to notice details about the grocery store in the book *Tom,* by Tomie dePaola.

THINKING CRITICALLY ABOUT THE TEXT

- What are some of the things Tom and Tommy like to do together?
- What are some of the lessons Tommy learns from his grandfather Tom?
- Describe the grocery store that Tom and Nana own—what is it like?
- What have you learned about butchers that you didn't know before?
- What have you learned about chickens that you didn't know before?
- How much trouble does Tommy *really* get into when he uses the chicken feet at school?

RESPONDING TO THE TEXT: INTEGRATED LANGUAGE ARTS

You will find that some of the activities listed in the literary guide for *Now One Foot, Now the Other* are also very appropriate to use with *Tom*. A few specific ideas for sharing *Tom* with your students are listed here.

Interviews

If your grandparents are alive, interview them about the work they do now or did when they were younger. Where do (did) they work? How long have they been working at their particular job? What is the work like? Do they enjoy what they do? Why did they choose their particular line of work? If your grandparents are not alive, see if one of your parents might be available. Interview a parent about one of his or her parents. Ask the same questions listed above.

Stories and Storytelling

Who shares stories with you—stories about the present or the past, or ones that are made up? Draw and write about someone who is your favorite storyteller.

You as the Storyteller!

The beauty of stories is that before there were books, stories were shared, told by one person to another or group of people. Share one of the special stories you have heard with someone else or a group of friends. Do they like the story as much as you liked hearing it in the first place?

22 ♥ On the Wing of a Whitebird

RESPONDING TO THE TEXT: WRITING

Recording Your Stories

Write about someone who has shared special stories with you and record some of the stories shared so that you don't forget them. You might keep these in a special journal or book and add favorite stories as you hear them from family members, friends, and others.

Practical Jokes

Did someone play a practical joke on you? Were you scared? Describe the situation, the joke or trick, and how you reacted. Did you tattle on the person? Did he or she get in trouble? Did you later think the trick was funny? Did you decide to play the trick on someone you know? Write about these experiences, describing the practical joke and joker, and share them with friends. Did any children have similar practical jokes played on them?

RESPONDING TO THE TEXT: ART

The Work Our Grandparents (or Special People) Do

Provide paper and any favorite art medium for children to draw a portrait of a grandparent or special person doing the work they do. Use the cover of *Tom* as an example for children. Note how Tomie dePaola placed his grandfather Tom in the setting of a butcher shop and included many details to show us exactly what the butcher shop was like. Children may need to interview grandparents or special people again to learn about details regarding their work setting. The finished art projects make wonderful gifts or can be displayed prior to a career day or a day celebrating special people at school.

RESPONDING TO THE TEXT: SCIENCE

Chicken Feet!

Invite a butcher from your local grocer or butcher shop to come and demonstrate how the tendons work on chicken feet. Consult with him or her first about what you want your children to see and experience during your classroom visit. Have children look closely at the tendons. Ask the butcher if he can pull the tendons to make the chicken feet open and close. Be ready for shrieks of delight! Encouraging children to use their senses once again, have them draw the chicken feet and describe how they look, feel, and smell.

Nana Upstairs & Nana Downstairs

SUMMARY

This first autobiographical book written by Tomie dePaola helps us learn about Tomie's special relationship with his grandmother, Nana Downstairs, and his great-grandmother, Nana Upstairs. Every Sunday, when Tommy was young, he would spend afternoons with both Nanas. He would run into the house and say hello to Nana Downstairs and then hurry upstairs to visit with Nana Upstairs, who was then ninety-four years old. They would both sit tied in chairs (so Nana wouldn't fall out) and share candy and stories. When Tommy learns from his mother that Nana Upstairs has died, he asks, "Won't she ever come back?" His mother answers gently, "No dear, except in your memory. She will come back in your memory whenever you think about her."

This book is the most gentle introduction I know for children to learn about the death of an elderly person. Originally published in 1973, it was completely redone in 1998 to celebrate the book's twenty-fifth year of publication. I suggest using either edition, but having access to both versions will add greatly to your discussions about Tomie dePaola's illustration techniques. Check your school or local library for the 1973 version.

PRE-READING ACTIVITIES

Gather children together and ask them if there is another home other than their own in which they spend special time, perhaps the home of a grandparent, aunt, or uncle. What is special about that place? What words come to mind that describe it?

MAKING PREDICTIONS

Show the covers of the book to your students and discuss:

- What is a Nana? Do you have one? What do you call her?
- Who do you think Nana Upstairs and Nana Downstairs are? Why do you think they are called that?

READING THE STORY

If you have both versions of the story, begin with the 1973 edition. Read through the story from beginning to end. Then, read the new version so you can compare the illustrations. The text remains the same, but the added touches of color in the 1998 edition are simply breathtaking.

THINKING CRITICALLY ABOUT THE TEXT

- Describe the special relationships that Tommy had with Nana Downstairs and with Nana Upstairs? How are they different and the same?
- What are some of the most important activities Tommy remembers sharing with his Nana Upstairs?
- Describe how young Tommy tries to figure out what "died" meant when he hears from his mother that Nana Upstairs has died.

Comparing Versions of *Nana Upstairs & Nana Downstairs*

Have a child assist you in holding one version of the book as you walk through the pages of both versions at the same time.

- What do children notice? How are the pages different or the same?
- Which version do they prefer?

SHARING PERSONAL EXPERIENCES

- Do you have any special relationships with relatives or friends, just like Tommy did with his Irish grandparents and great-grandmother? Who are these special people in your life?
- Do you know any relative or friend who has died?
- How did someone comfort you or help you feel better about the person dying?

RESPONDING TO THE TEXT: INTEGRATED LANGUAGE ARTS

Presenting . . . Special Times!

Tommy spent each Sunday afternoon with Nana Upstairs sitting side by side in chairs, eating candy, and telling stories. She was his best friend when he was four years old. Is there a special relative or friend that comes to mind after listening to this part of the story? Is that person living or has she or he passed away? Who is that person? Do you have special activities or traditions that you participate in regularly together? Think about how you might share that special relative or friend with your classmates through some kind of simple presentation. Can you bring in a photo or draw a picture of the person? You might bring in an object that belongs to that person or a gift you received from him or her. Have a wonderful time sharing your special friend with others. If the person is still alive, you might ask him or her to come in for the presentation itself.

Falling Stars

Shortly after Nana Upstairs dies, Tommy looks out the window and sees a falling star. His mother tells him that "perhaps that was a kiss from Nana Upstairs." Have you ever seen a falling star? How have falling stars been explained to you? Draw or paint one if you like and share any explanation you may have for them.

RESPONDING TO THE TEXT: WRITING

When I Was Four . . .

Tomie dePaola wrote this story remembering clearly what life was like for him when he was four years old. Do you remember something that happened to you when you were four or something you liked to do all the time at that age? If not, ask your parents if they can help you with some ideas or details. Write (or dictate, with younger children) a short story describing the activities you liked to participate in when you were four. You might continue the story starter, "When I was four, I . . ."

When I Am Ninety-four . . .

Encourage children to try to fathom all that they may have seen and done if they lived to be ninety-four. What are some of the things they think they may have done? Will they go to college, get married, have children, have pets, travel, work? What will their career be? Invite them to think about all the stories they think they might be able to share with a four-year-old grandchild when *they* are ninety-four! Have them share these thoughts with friends in the classroom. Children might want to try to draw themselves when they are ninety-four—these drawings may prove to be hysterical.

RESPONDING TO THE TEXT: ART

Remembering Those We Love

Sometimes when we are sad, it is often hard to put our feelings into words. After reading *Nana Upstairs & Nana Downstairs* you might simply provide paper and colored pencils or crayons for children to draw on as they listen to some quiet music. They may want to draw pictures of those people or pets they have lost in their lives, or they may not. Children may choose to draw pictures of people who are alive and for whom they are thankful.

"Kisses from"—Cards of Good Cheer

Children may choose to draw or paint beautiful scenes on little cards to present to people who are special in their lives or those who might need a little cheer.

Thinking about You Cards . . .

You may want your class to participate in a project in which they create cards for men and women who are in the armed forces, sending their love, support, and good cheer.

Watch Out for the Chicken Feet in Your Soup

SUMMARY

Joey and his friend Eugene go to visit Joey's grandmother at her home. Joey warns Eugene that his Italian grandmother is "always cooking and talks funny." He is embarrassed by his grandmother, thinking she is so different. Joey and Eugene arrive at the very traditional Italian home of Nana, where life is so different and special that Eugene just can't help commenting and asking questions about everything. He loves the food and Nana notices. She even invites Eugene to help her bake her special bread. Joey puts on quite a good pout until at the end, Nana presents Joey with a special bread doll, reminding him that he is her "special Joey."

This story is autobiographical in that Tomie dePaola is "Joey" in the story. We learn what it may have been like to visit the home of Tomie's "Nana Fall-River," who lived in Fall River, Massachusetts. She is very Italian and we get a glimpse into traditional Italian homes by noticing all of the details in Tomie dePaola's artwork.

PRE-READING ACTIVITIES: EXPERIENCING OTHER CULTURES

Create a graph with children by asking children if they have participated in any multicultural experiences. For instance, have any of them been to festivities to celebrate Cinco de Mayo, Chinese New Year, or other holidays special to other cultures? Perhaps your school's locale is home to particular ethnic cultures. Brainstorm a list of various multicultural celebrations, and create a graph like the one below to note who has or has not had experiences outside of their own culture.

Cinco de Mayo	Chinese New Year	Las Posadas	Other

MAKING PREDICTIONS

Open the book so children can see both the front and back covers. Explain that this is a book about a particular culture of people, but that many things in the pictures will remind them of their own homes and families.

- What do children notice about the cover?
- Do the illustrations depict an unusual place or could this be a picture of anyone's house?
- What do you think it means to "watch out for the chicken feet in your soup?"

READING THE STORY

Stop after reading the first introduction page: "Now, listen Eugene, my grandma is nice. But she pinches my cheeks a lot and her house is full of funny old stuff. She's always cooking and she talks funny, too. And, Eugene . . ." This is something not commonly found in children's books. Rarely do authors set the tone and give a little introduction before the actual story begins.

Now, read the story with the children, taking time to point out all of the details in the illustrations.

THINKING CRITICALLY ABOUT THE TEXT

- How would you describe Eugene's experience of Nana?
- How would Eugene describe Nana, her home, and the food she prepares for him and Joey?
- How would you describe Joey's behavior? Why do you think he acts the way he does?

SHARING PERSONAL EXPERIENCES

- Does this book remind you of any special people in your life? Do any of your relatives speak another language regularly or have special traditions that they share with you when you visit?
- Have you ever been embarrassed by one of your relatives or friends because they act a little different? How do you react when introducing these people to friends?

RESPONDING TO THE TEXT: INTEGRATED LANGUAGE ARTS

Cooking and Sharing Bread

Some ideas for cooking and eating experiences are:

- Use the bread dolls recipe at the back of the book to create your own bread dolls and then have children write about the process. What did they do first, next, last?
- Encourage children to bring in other favorite bread recipes and make one or more of them. Why are these recipes special?

- Bring in several different types of bread, made in various countries or in the style of those countries, and have a taste comparison. After children try each type of bread, encourage them to discuss what they like or do not like about the particular type of bread. Examples of possible breads to bring in include flatbread, tortillas, challah, sourdough, and Irish soda bread.

RESPONDING TO THE TEXT: MATH

Graphing Chicken Soup

Have children share their preferences for the kind of chicken soup they prefer. Create a simple graph like the one below.

Chicken Noodle	Chicken with Rice	Homemade Chicken Noodle

RESPONDING TO THE TEXT: ART

Special Treasures

There are many special treasures displayed in Nana's house. What is a special treasure on display at your house? Choose one to draw and write about. If you can, try to take a picture of it and bring the photo in to share with the rest of the class. Are some of your family's special treasures the same or similar to those of someone else?

Silhouettes

Hanging on the wall in Nana Fall-River's dining room, Tomie has created some silhouettes, most likely of other relatives. Ask children if they have even seen a silhouette. Take a photo of each child's profile and after developing and printing the photos, have children create a simple silhouette of their own. You might use a copy machine to enlarge the photos for tracing for younger children or have older children use the profiles as they are to enlarge and sketch their own. Transfer these onto black construction paper before matting them. These make a wonderful gift for parents.

RESPONDING TO THE TEXT: DRAMA

Sharing Family Activities

Cooking is a special activity that many families participate in together. Do you cook with your family? Does your family have any special activities they do together? What are they? Using pantomime, take turns acting out some of the simple or special activities you and your family participate in regularly. Examples might be eating family meals together, baking cookies, going to ball games, putting puzzles together, eating popcorn, and watching movies.

The Baby Sister

SUMMARY

Tommy is so excited when his mom tells him that she is going to have a baby. "Can I have a baby sister with a red ribbon in her hair?" Tommy asks his mom. When Tommy's mom finally goes to the hospital, it is Tommy's Italian Grandmother, Nana Fall-River, not his beloved Aunt Nell, who comes to stay for a week to take care of Tommy and his brother Joe. Tommy and Nana don't exactly get along because Nana tends to be stern with him. Tommy stops eating and just sits around and pouts, until one day Tommy sees his mom wave from her hospital window. She tells Tommy that she will be home soon and to be good for Nana Fall-River. Tommy agrees and goes home to reconcile with Nana. Together they greet Tommy's little sister upon her arrival home, complete with a red ribbon in her hair.

PRE-READING ACTIVITIES

What do your students think about siblings? Ask them to share the pros and cons of having a brother, sister, or more than one sibling? What do the children who have no siblings think? Would they like to have a brother or sister if they could? Why or why not?

MAKING PREDICTIONS

- Looking at the front cover of the book, how do you think Tommy feels about his baby sister?
- Many of us have baby sisters. How do you think this story will be different from any of our own stories about our baby sisters?

READING THE STORY

Read *The Baby Sister* slowly, letting children notice the differences in artwork that Tomie dePaola uses throughout this book.

THINKING CRITICALLY ABOUT THE TEXT

- What are some of the ways Tommy's family prepares for the arrival of the baby?
- How does Tommy help out?
- Why does Tommy have problems with Nana Fall-River?
- Why can't Tommy visit his mother in the hospital?
- Why does Tommy change his behavior with Nana?
- Describe the homecoming celebration for Tommy's baby sister. What are the most special moments?

SHARING PERSONAL EXPERIENCES

- Do you have a baby brother or sister?
- What do you remember about any preparations your family made to get ready for the baby's arrival?

- Do you remember when the baby arrived at your home? How did you greet your baby sister or brother?

RESPONDING TO THE TEXT: INTEGRATED LANGUAGE ARTS

My Brother/Sister Is Special Because . . .

Children draw and write about a brother or sister. They might share a funny or special story about him or her. Provide time for children to brainstorm ideas for these stories first, before writing and illustrating them. For those children who have more than one sibling, they could write and illustrate a short story about each one. For those children without siblings, they could write about someone in their life who is like a sibling—a cousin or friend perhaps.

RESPONDING TO THE TEXT: WRITING

Baby Poems

Encourage your students to write a poem or a short description of a baby they know, whether it is a family member or a friend's baby. When they are done, give each child a small card to write the baby poem on. Encourage children to share their writings with one another. Do any particular words stand out when children describe babies, like cute or tiny? Display the poems on a small bulletin board.

What Babies Like to Do

Using the following form, have children complete the lines prompting what they think babies like to do.

Babies like to: _____

_____

_____

and _____

RESPONDING TO THE TEXT: ART

Creating a Photo Collage

Tomie dePaola begins *The Baby Sister* with drawings of a photo collage of important family members. Encourage children to create their own family collage by drawing pictures of family members on 3" × 5" index cards or ones cut smaller. Children could sketch these in pencil and then matte them on another color, or include color in their sketched "photos." If you have access to photo tabs, they will accentuate the display of each child's collage.

RESPONDING TO THE TEXT: MATH

Human Graphing Exercise

Before beginning this exercise, use large index cards (5" × 8") to quickly create graph signs needed (see illustration below).

No siblings	1 sibling	2 sibling	3 sibling	4 or more siblings

Invite all of your students to stand up near their tables or desks. Organize them through the following:

- Ask students, "Who has brothers or sisters?" and ask those who do to move to a designated part of the classroom.
- Ask how many students have siblings (check for understanding with the children regarding the use of this word) and how many do not? Give children the opportunity to count themselves.
- Ask students who have a sibling to discuss among themselves and decide who has the most siblings and who has the least. Using a line you have put down with tape on the floor or a carpet edge, encourage children to create a human graph with their bodies, beginning with those who have the fewest siblings to those who have the most. Have the children who have one sibling stand in one line, those who have two siblings line up next to them, and so on.
- Ask the children who don't have siblings to line up on the other side of those who have one sibling.
- Now ask all children to sit down in their rows so all of them can see the human graph more clearly.

The human graph from above might look something like this:

Record a simple graph like the one shown here on the board near your human graph so that the students can see and compare one column of the human graph to the others. Ask:

```
                X
  X             X
  X             X         X
  X             X    X    X
  X             X    X    X    X
  ―――――――――――――――――――――――――――――――――
  0             1    2    3    4    more
```

each X = 1 child

- Are there more children *with* siblings in our classroom or *without*?
- Are there more classmates with two siblings or more classmates with one brother or sister? Ask any other questions relevant to your particular classroom sibling graph.

As a written record, you might give older children graph paper with 1" squares to record the sibling graph. Each child could circle where they sat on the human graph. This could be the beginning of several human graphs that you do throughout the school year.

Chapter 2

The *Strega Nona* Series

INTRODUCTION

There has been much confusion about the origin of the *Strega Nona* stories. Many people of Italian descent claim that *Strega Nona* is a retelling of an old Italian folktale their grandmothers told them when they were growing up. Impossible! Strega Nona is an original character created by Tomie dePaola. She was conceived as Tomie was doodling (everyone thought he was taking meticulous notes) during a staff meeting at the college where he was teaching. The sketch remained on Tomie's wall for some time until the idea of Strega Nona came to him. Tomie's inspiration for the *Strega Nona* stories came from tales such as "The Magic Porridge Pot" and "The Sorcerer's Apprentice." Of course, he was also inspired by his Italian heritage and so he placed Strega Nona in an Italian setting.

Special Note: Since Strega Nona means "Grandma Witch" in Italian, only you can decide whether this is going to be an issue to the parents of the children you teach. All of my experiences with children indicate that they know Strega Nona as a kindly, old grandmotherly-like person who goes about treating each person she meets with love. Presented as such, there have been no problems.

If you need to preface your reading of the stories, you might want to share with your students that in a town in Calabria in southern Italy, Strega Nona is the beloved old woman who everyone goes to when they have troubles. Although her name means "Grandma Witch," it is actually *love* that Strega Nona uses to help "cure" people's ailments. Back in the time when there were no doctors, Strega Nona's use of herbs and tenderness were just what people needed when they came to her house for help.

Tomie dePaola has written eight stories about Strega Nona to date and he has another book in process at this time. Strega Nona is perhaps the most famous and beloved of all of Tomie dePaola's characters and she is shared in classrooms and libraries all around the world. My goal in writing literary guides for the *Strega Nona* stories is to provide rich literary response ideas for you to choose from and share with your children after reading the books.

There is no right way to enjoy Tomie dePaola's *Strega Nona* stories. You may choose to share *Strega Nona* with your children but not have time to share the other seven stories. Then again, many teachers may choose to do a full unit based on all eight stories about Strega Nona. There are more than enough ideas to choose from to personalize a *Strega Nona* unit that is right for you.

I weave one particular activity throughout all eight literary guides. I provide ideas for you and your students to create a mural of Strega Nona's village in Calabria, Italy. In addition, puppet making ideas are included so that children can create puppets to use in front of the mural. I hope you will have fun with this activity.

The goal is for you to have fun getting to know Strega Nona, Big Anthony, Bambolona, and all of the characters in the *Strega Nona* stories. Enjoy all of the stories and you will learn "everything you need to become a true strega. You have everything you need. You have the spirit and kindness that comes from the heart . . . And when I tell you the *ingrediente segreto*—the secret ingredient . . . then you will be not only a true strega, but a great one!"

Strega Nona

SUMMARY

Strega Nona, the grandmotherly "old witch" that everyone in Calabria goes to when they have troubles, is getting old and needs some help. She posts a notice in the town square for an assistant and Big Anthony answers it. Big Anthony, who always means well but never really pays attention, begins to work for Strega Nona. Strega Nona gives Big Anthony strict orders never to touch her pasta pot. But Big Anthony is curious, and one day he overhears Strega Nona singing to her magical pasta pot as it bubbles and boils and creates their pasta dinner. When he tells some of the townspeople the next day about Strega Nona's "magical" pasta pot, they think he is lying to them. Big Anthony becomes very angry and vows that "someday I will get the pasta pot and make it cook." He gets his opportunity two days later when Strega Nona travels to see her friend Strega Amelia. When Big Anthony invites all of the townspeople to see how he made the magic pasta pot work, everyone is very impressed and Big Anthony is a hero until he cannot make the magic pasta pot stop making pasta! Discover with your children the secret of the pasta pot, as Strega Nona returns just in time to save Big Anthony and all of the townspeople.

PRE-READING ACTIVITIES

Find Calabria

The region of Calabria is at the tip of the boot-shaped country. The capital of Calabria is Reggio di Calabria. The story takes place in an unnamed town in Calabria. Try to locate it on a map of Italy or on a map of the world.

Before There Were Doctors . . .

Help your students think of times when there was no medicine or doctors available. Some of them may know about the Oregon Trail or other adventures where doctors or those who had learned from doctors used plants and other remedies made from vegetables (e.g., onion poultices) to help sick people along the way.

MAKING PREDICTIONS

Show both the front and back covers of *Strega Nona* to your children and point out the title of the book. Discuss:

- Does the name of the book sound familiar to you?
- Have you ever heard of someone being called a *Strega* before? or Nona?

- Where do you think this story takes place?
- What do you notice about the buildings on the cover? the roofs? the doorways and windows?
- There is a large, round silver circle on the cover. What do you think that is?

Discuss the Caldecott Medal and its importance. The Caldecott Honor is an award given in the United States each year to outstanding illustrated children's books. Tomie dePaola won the Caldecott Honor Medal for *Strega Nona* in 1975.

READING THE STORY

Read *Strega Nona* with your children. Take time to savor the detailed award-winning illustrations done by Tomie dePaola.

THINKING CRITICALLY ABOUT THE TEXT

- How would you describe Strega Nona? You might want to make a list of words that describe her to post and add to as you read several of the *Strega Nona* books.
- What are some of the ways Strega Nona helps people in her town in Calabria?
- Do you know anyone in your life who is similar to Strega Nona?
- What words would you use to describe Big Anthony? You may want to begin listing words on chart paper that describe Big Anthony.
- Does the story take place during the present time or in the past? How can you tell?
- Why do you think Big Anthony tells the townspeople about the magic pasta pot?
- Why is Big Anthony determined to make the pasta pot cook?
- Why does he disobey Strega Nona?
- "The punishment must fit the crime," says Strega Nona, when the townspeople want to punish Big Anthony. What do you think that means?

SHARING PERSONAL EXPERIENCES

- Big Anthony just can't resist trying out Strega Nona's pasta pot. Was there ever a time when you disobeyed someone because you just couldn't resist something? What happened?
- Was there a time when you were really attracted to doing or taking something you weren't supposed to and you resisted? How did you manage to control your urges and behavior? How were you able to resist the people or things that were tempting you?

RESPONDING TO THE TEXT: INTEGRATED LANGUAGE ARTS

Retelling the Story

Have children write the story with partners, telling what happened in their own words. Challenge them to try to use only ten sentences to retell what happened in the story.

Rewriting the Ending

What would have happened if Strega Nona had not returned in time? What would have happened to Big Anthony? the townspeople? Have children rewrite the ending to the story using their vivid imaginations and using the great gift of exaggeration used in the story.

RESPONDING TO THE TEXT: WRITING

Writing about Personal Events

Have children write about times when they were tempted to do something and resisted. You could have them divide papers in half and label them as follows:

I really wanted to do this:	This is what I did instead (or had to do):

Getting in Touch with Strega Nona

There were no cars or phones back in the time of Strega Nona. Ask your children to brainstorm ways the townspeople could have gotten in touch with Strega Nona, who was visiting her friend Strega Amelia in the town over the mountain. Have children draw or write their idea on a piece of paper and put it on a chart that shows:

Transportation now:	Transportation then:

Making Get Well Cards for Big Anthony

Have children use various art mediums—drawing, painting, or pop-up techniques—to make a get well card for Big Anthony. Help them brainstorm funny sayings for the front of the card and include a picture of Big Anthony after eating too much pasta.

Using Rubber Stamps

The Kidstamps Company has created a set of Strega Nona rubber stamps. Children can use the stamps to:

- retell the story (with or without words).
- rewrite the ending, using the stamps to begin the story, then adding their own illustrations.
- create their own Strega Nona stories.
- create get well cards for Big Anthony.
- add "talking bubbles" or "thinking bubbles" to the characters in order to have them share things they might be saying under their breath or thinking to themselves.

RESPONDING TO THE TEXT: DRAMA

Create a Puppet Play

Use the ideas in the Art response section (next page) to assist children in creating their own background mural and puppets to put on a puppet show of *Strega Nona*.

Note: You might want to think ahead and decide if you are going to use all of the *Strega Nona* stories in your class. If so, you can divide children into committees and have each committee concentrate on creating the puppets for each of the stories. So there would be a *Strega Nona* committee, a *Big Anthony and the Magic Ring* committee, and so on, for each story. Committees could also work on helping plan and create parts of the mural that are essential to their story.

Readers Theatre

Students can do an informal readers theatre performance of the story, with several children narrating the story. The speaking parts can be read by children playing the parts of:

Strega Nona	a sister from the convent
Big Anthony	the mayor
	townspeople

Children holding the above parts would read them during the narration as their speaking parts occur. If they wish, children could also make props or wear costumes. The narration would need to be divided among several children, as the story is quite long, or you could choose one section of the book for children to share. The fun and learning occur through the reading of the story line, attending to the punctuation, inflection of voices, and children getting ready to read their parts. Another option is for the remaining children to pantomime or act out the story while the reading is done. The more children you can involve, the better!

RESPONDING TO THE TEXT: ART

Drawing and Painting "*Stregas*"

In the video *A Visit with Tomie dePaola,* Tomie shares how he draws Strega Nona, always beginning with her kerchief. Watch this section of the video if you have the chance and have children observe

Tomie drawing and painting this beloved character in his books. Following the video, your students may want to draw and paint their own rendition of Strega Nona or create their very own *Strega* or *Stregone* (a male *Strega*). Give them pencils, watercolors, and fine-tipped markers for drawing, painting, and outlining their own *Stregas*.

Make a Mural (and Possible Backdrop)

Help children plan out and paint a mural for the classroom that depicts Strega Nona's village in Calabria. Have them use the book to study and design the houses with beautiful tile roofs, the town square, the hills, and background. To make a three-dimensional mural, children could use milk cartons to create houses in the town (painted or covered with paper) and then attach them to the mural. Or you can glue children's drawings or paintings to thin boxes and attach the boxes to the mural to create a three-dimensional effect. This mural could be used as a backdrop for puppet plays your students act out using all of the *Strega Nona* stories. (See *note* in the Drama response section above.)

Note: If you are going to have your children read and enjoy several *Strega Nona* stories and create a mural to use throughout their reading, you will want children to include the following in their mural plan:

- Strega Nona's house, inside and out
- the village square
- the convent
- the church (which could be located near the convent)
- the countryside
- a road or path leading to and from the town
- extra room for various buildings and landscapes that appear in other *Strega Nona* stories.

Make *Strega Nona* Puppets

Using whatever medium children are comfortable with, have children work together to make puppets of Strega Nona, Big Anthony, the mayor, and some of the townspeople. With younger children I like to use the following method. You will need:

- a piece of 3" × 5" tag board or thin, wooden scrap rectangle for each child.
- tag board scraps to make arms and legs.
- one old ruler or paint stirrer for each puppet (paint stores might donate stirrers).
- fabric scraps and decorative trims.
- yarn.
- white glue.
- wood glue, if attaching wood scraps to the paint stirrers or rulers, although school glue will also work.

1. Use an old ruler or paint stirrer as a base for each puppet.
2. Using regular or wood glue, have children attach one 3" × 5" tag board or thin wooden scrap as a body base to their ruler or paint stirrer.
3. Use tag board scraps to make arms, legs, and a head for the puppet. Attach them to the body with glue.

4. Using fabric scraps and trims, have children create clothing for the characters from *Strega Nona*. Have each child attach the clothing to the railroad board or wooden base they have previously created.

5. Add hair by using yarn scraps and attaching with them glue.

The length of the wooden stirrers will work perfectly if your students use the mural as a backdrop for acting out the *Strega Nona* stories or stories they make up on their own. The back of the puppet may look something like the sample shown on the next page.

When your puppets are done, have children act out the story using their puppets and the mural as a backdrop.

RESPONDING TO THE TEXT: PASTA ART

Pasta comes in such wonderful shapes and sizes. Children can bring in different kinds of pasta they have at home and use it in a variety of art projects.

Create a 3-D Dinner

Children can create their own three-dimensional plate of pasta using a simple paper dinner plate or piece of tag board. Have children arrange a plate of their favorite kinds of pasta for themselves. Have them glue the pasta down using regular white school glue or have an adult assist children using a glue gun. Then, using a bottle of white glue that has been colored with paint (three parts white glue and one part paint), assist children in squirting glue over the pasta to represent their favorite sauce. When dry, display each child's creation. Ask children to label their pasta dishes and share them with others.

Use Colored Pasta for Math Projects, Artwork, and Jewelry

Use small amounts of food coloring and rubbing alcohol in a jar to create colored pasta that can be used in numerous art and math projects. (I pour enough rubbing alcohol to cover the bottom of a glass mayonnaise jar and then add several drops of food coloring. I throw in some pasta to test the color and either add more alcohol or food coloring depending on the depth of color needed.) Pasta necklaces, pasta pictures, and pasta patterning are just some of the activities you can do with children using colored pasta. Young children love to sort and string colored macaroni or other pasta for wonderful creations to wear.

You will already have many favorite ideas of your own on how to use pasta in art projects for children. Ask your children for their ideas too!

Create Decorative Frames and Containers

Use various kinds of pasta to decorate pencil cans and picture frames. Children glue on the pasta and then spray paint the whole object.

Create an Artistic Pasta Pin

Using pasta, tag board, glue, and paint, create a pasta pin. Let children work with several pieces of pasta to create a pleasing arrangement. Have them glue the pasta onto a small rectangle or square of tag or railroad board using school glue or a quick-sticking glue. (I use $1\frac{1}{2}" \times 2"$ rectangles cut out of recycled cardboard boxes for my pins.) Choose a color to spray paint the pin (I used gold paint) and have an adult

♥♥♥ — ♥♥♥ — ♥♥♥ — ♥♥♥ — ♥♥♥ — ♥♥♥

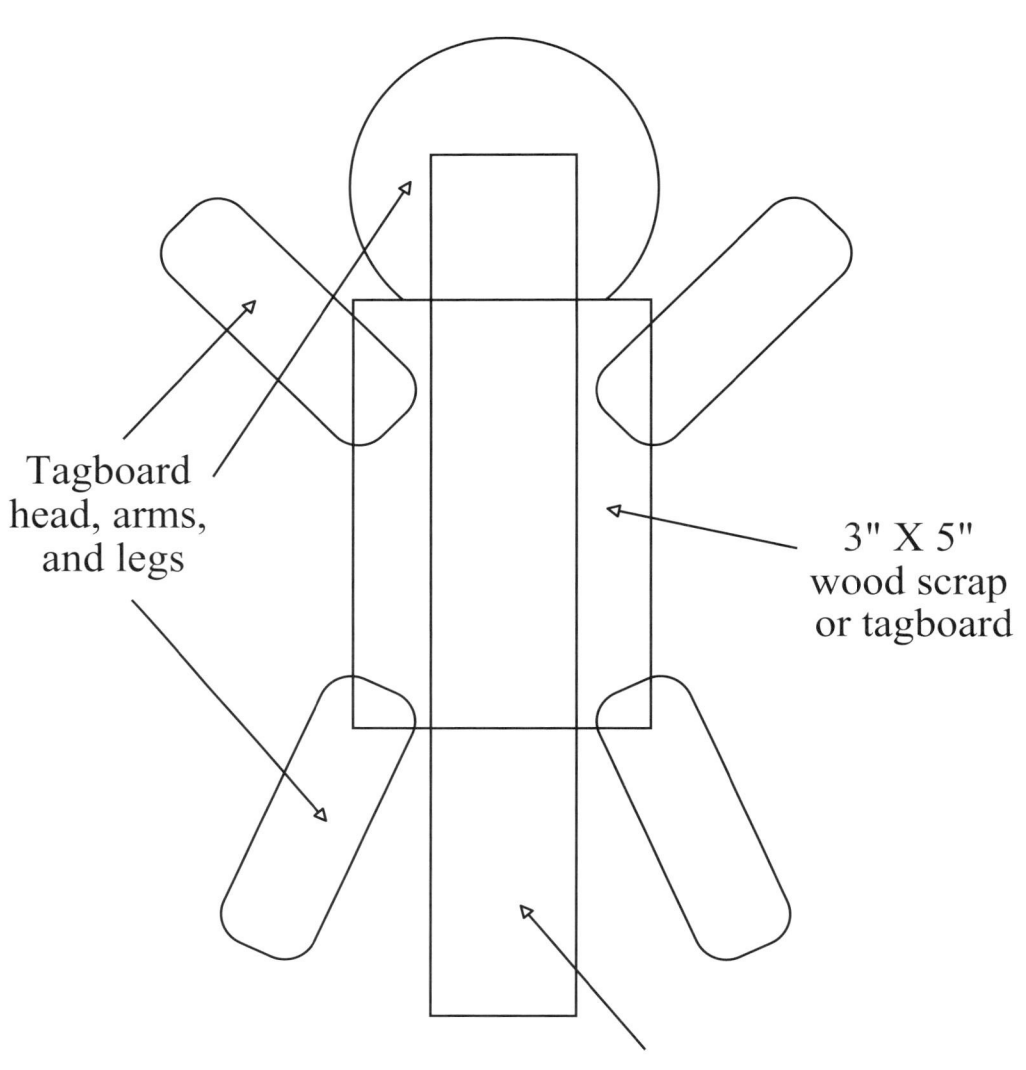

Tagboard head, arms, and legs

3" X 5" wood scrap or tagboard

Paint stirrer

♥♥♥ — ♥♥♥ — ♥♥♥ — ♥♥♥ — ♥♥♥ — ♥♥♥

do the spraying. When the pins are dry, add additional sparkle if desired with sequins and little trims. Have an adult use a glue gun or jewelry glue to attach a pin on the back of each child's creation.

Create a Pasta Chart

Many poster, cooking, or specialty grocery stores sell posters that have a variety of pastas illustrated. Use the poster to help children learn what the different types of pasta and shapes are called and to learn some simple Italian words. Then, invite children to bring in different types of pasta and begin making your own classroom pasta chart. Using glue and a piece of tag board, create a chart of the pastas, putting them in alphabetical order and labeling them. Children will have fun learning some of the Italian names and their meanings.

RESPONDING TO THE TEXT: COOKING

Your school may have limitations on cooking, but perhaps some of these ideas will work for you.

Making Pasta

Before you make and share pasta, have your children graph their choice of toppings on a simple graph—What kind of sauce would you like with your pasta? Create spaces on the graph for each child to sign his or her name below the topping of his or her choice. (This will help you in purchasing or gathering the ingredients for your pasta celebration.)

Boil up a large pot of pasta—enough for each child to have a small portion. Using paper bowls, plastic forks, and plastic spoons, teach children how to twirl the pasta around their forks using a spoon as a base. Explain to them that this is how they eat pasta in Italy.

What kind of sauce would you like with your pasta?

Butter only	Butter and parmesan	Tomato sauce

Learn How Pasta Is Made

Using books on the subject, or by doing some research on the Internet, assist children in learning how pasta is made and produced in large quantities. Then, if you have a local pasta store, invite a pasta maker to speak with your children about how fresh pasta is made. If you are able, make simple pasta with your children. A nice recipe for making pasta with children can be found in the *Kids' Multicultural Cookbook,* by Deanna Cook.

Sharing Pasta Favorites—A Classroom Newsletter or Recipe Book

Have children share what they have learned about pasta as well as their favorite kinds of pasta and sauces. Ask each child to bring in their favorite recipe from home, having a parent check the copied recipe for accuracy (I've learned from experience). If you have a willing and resourceful parent, ask him or her to type up the information children share and all of the recipes they bring in. Bind them into a classroom pasta newsletter or cookbook. This could be a wonderful holiday gift for parents. To make a cover, children could arrange different-shaped pasta on construction paper and spray paint over it to create an original pasta creation.

Other Italian Favorites

You might invite any Italian relatives of your children to share some of their favorite Italian foods with the class. Or, perhaps someone from a local Italian market would be willing to come in and talk with your students about unusual and/or typical Italian foods they might not know about.

You can find original Italian recipes from Tomie dePaola in some of his other books. In *Watch Out for the Chicken Feet in Your Soup,* Tomie provides a recipe for making bread dolls. In *Jingle, the Christmas Clown,* there is a recipe to make Donna Chiara's Stelline d'Oro. Tomie dePaola has also illustrated an Italian cookbook written by his good friend Mary Ann Esposito, entitled *Celebrations, Italian Style,* which has many Italian recipes.

RESPONDING TO THE TEXT: MATH

Sorting Pasta Shapes

Invite each child to bring in a cup or plastic bag full of pasta that they have at home or find at their local market. Have them sort the pasta by shape, size, color, grooves, and thickness. As a challenge, you could ask each child to write and describe one piece of pasta and have the other children guess which one he or she is describing. Children will need to be very detailed in their descriptions in order for the others to identify it.

Weighing Pasta

With the various pastas your children bring in, have them take thirty to thirty-five pieces and weigh them. Using a scale that can measure ounces, compare the differences between pastas. If you don't have access to a scale, compare pasta weights using unifix cubes, tiles, or wooden cubes as your unit of measure. Record the comparisons on a chart for all to see. For an interesting, additional comparison, cook one type of pasta with the class and then weigh it again. Does it weigh the same as the dry type of pasta? Why or why not?

| 1/2" | 3/4" | 1" | 1-1/4" | 1-1/2" |

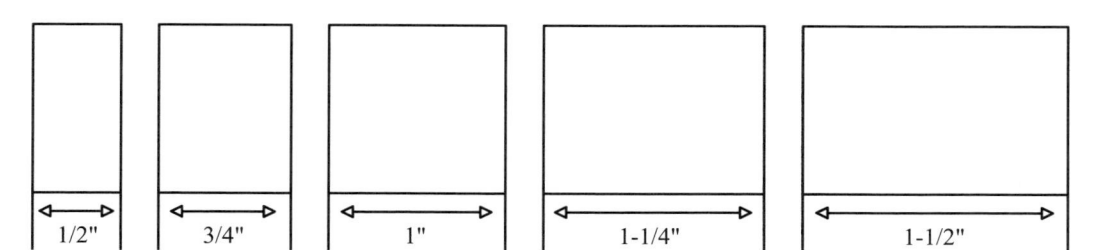

Measuring Pasta

Older children can use a ruler to measure the lengths of pieces of pasta to the nearest half or quarter inch. Be sure to provide everything from little elbow macaroni to lasagna noodles for comparison. Children may even want to glue down the pieces of pasta on a chart and list the measurements they have found. If you don't have enough pasta for children to do this individually, have them work in groups to make their charts, checking with each other to make sure they agree on the measurements.

Big Anthony and the Magic Ring

SUMMARY

It is the beginning of springtime, there are birds in the air and flowers are blooming on the hillsides. Everything is routine around Strega Nona's house. People are still coming to see her with their problems and Bambolona, the baker's daughter, still delivers bread to her each day. However, Big Anthony, Strega Nona's assistant, has spring fever and is dragging his feet everywhere, not completing his chores, and sleeping late. Strega Nona suggests that he go to the village dance that night for some excitement.

Strega Nona thinks about her own suggestion to Big Anthony and decides to go to the dance herself. But first, she digs around to find her magic ring. Using it (and of course, Big Anthony secretly sees her), Strega Nona turns herself into a beautiful young woman. Big Anthony follows Strega Nona into the village where he watches her dance the tarantella with handsome men all evening. Vowing to get his hands on the ring, he waits for his chance. The very next day, Strega Nona goes to visit her godchildren and Big Anthony seizes the opportunity to use the magic ring. He puts on the ring, turns into Handsome Big Anthony, and goes into the town where all of the women beg to dance with him. He loves it!

But when Handsome Big Anthony becomes tired of dancing, the women won't let him stop. Frantically, he tries to get away from them and tries to get the ring off of his finger, but it's stuck! Read with your students to find out how Handsome Big Anthony is saved from being pushed, shoved, grabbed, and kissed endlessly and how he is changed back into regular Big Anthony once again.

PRE-READING ACTIVITIES

Special Person for a Day

Have your ever wished you could be someone else for just a day? Who is it and why would you like to be that person? Have your students share their reasons for "walking in another person's shoes" for a day.

Spring Fever Stories

What are some signs you notice when spring is in the air? What are those signs? Help children make a "Signs of Spring web." It might look something like this:

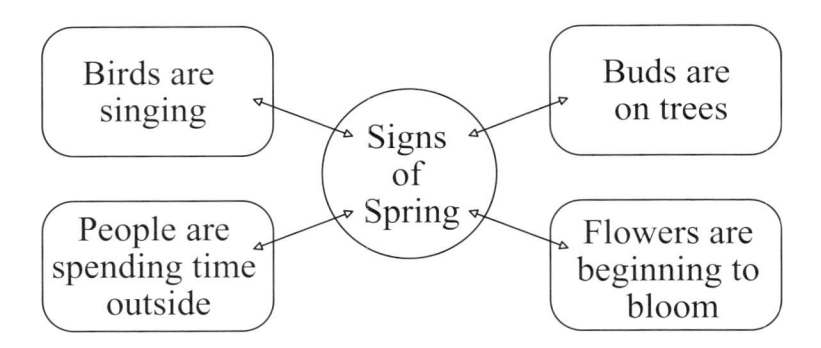

```
    Birds are              Buds are
    singing                on trees
              Signs
                of
              Spring
  People are              Flowers are
 spending time            beginning to
   outside                   bloom
```

MAKING PREDICTIONS

Show both the front and back covers of *Big Anthony and the Magic Ring* to your children and discuss:

- What do you remember about Big Anthony from the first story we read about Strega Nona?
- What do you think *Big Anthony and the Magic Ring* is about?
- Why might Big Anthony need or find a magic ring?
- Do you think the setting (where the story takes place) is the same as in *Strega Nona*? Why or why not? (You may need to bring out your copy of *Strega Nona* for comparison.)

READING THE STORY

Read *Big Anthony and the Magic Ring* with your children.

Predicting within the Story

You may want to stop at the point where Handsome Big Anthony has climbed to the top of a cypress tree and the ladies begin to shake it. When they have shaken the tree so hard that Handsome Big Anthony loses his grip and flies through the air, ask your children:

- Where do you think Handsome Big Anthony will land?
- What do you think is going to happen to him now?

THINKING CRITICALLY ABOUT THE TEXT

- Who is Bambolona? Why do you think Big Anthony doesn't notice her?
- At the beginning of the story, how is Big Anthony different from his usual self?
- What characteristics of Big Anthony are the same as in the first *Strega Nona* story?
- Does "the punishment fit the crime" for Big Anthony in this story as it does in *Strega Nona*? Why or why not?

- How is the song/spell that Strega Nona and Big Anthony sing when using the magic ring different than the song used in *Strega Nona*?
- At the end of the story, Big Anthony tells Strega Nona, ". . . you saved my life. Never again, I promise—never will I touch your magic." Do you believe him? Why or why not?
- Strega Nona answers Big Anthony, "Never mind, Big Anthony. There are other kinds of magic in the spring?" What do you think she means?
- Can we add any additional words to our lists that describe Strega Nona and Big Anthony? What words would you add based on our reading *Big Anthony and the Magic Ring*?
- Add Bambolona's name to the list. How would you describe her?

SHARING PERSONAL EXPERIENCES

Have your parents or an adult ever told you, "Oh———, you will never learn!" Allow children to share their stories with one another. If you remember a time when someone in your life said that to you, begin by sharing your story with the students.

RESPONDING TO THE TEXT: INTEGRATED LANGUAGE ARTS

In the Winter I Can . . . In the Spring I Can . . .

On one side of a thin paper plate children draw and write about something they can do only in the wintertime. Then, on the other side, they draw and label an activity they can do only in the springtime. These drawings can be hung like mobiles above children's desks.

Bambolona and the Ring

What if Bambolona was granted permission to use Strega Nona's magic ring? Write about and draw how you think she would like to change herself.

Wishes, Wishes, Wishes

Sometimes what we wish for and what we receive are two different things. Write about a time you received something that you wished or hoped for and it didn't turn out like you expected. Or, perhaps, what you wished for turned out to be more of a problem than a delight, like Big Anthony's changing into Handsome Big Anthony. Write and draw about this experience.

RESPONDING TO THE TEXT: WRITING

My Favorite Things to Do in the Spring

Children write about what they love to do in the springtime. You might have children refer to the Signs of Spring web they created earlier in the unit to give them ideas for their writing.

A Daily Schedule

Children write about a person they might like to be for a day, stating why they would like to be that person. Then, have each child create an hour-by-hour schedule of what he or she would do for the day.

Create a Chant or Song to Sing

Create your own magic rings and a chant or song to sing as you use it. After children think about someone else they would like to be for a day, or a way they are changed or improved, have them create a song or chant to say with their very own magic ring. Have each child write a before and after chant—one that changes them somehow and then returns them to their normal self.

Removing Rings

Strega Nona used olive oil to loosen the ring on Handsome Big Anthony's finger so he could take it off. Have your children ask their parents, grandparents, or other special adults about other tricks or "remedies" they have used to get rings off when they were too tight.

What If Big Anthony Found the Wrong Ring?

Have children return to the part in the story where Big Anthony rummages through the drawers of Strega Nona's cupboard. What if he accidentally found the wrong ring? What might it do? Would the ring do anything when Big Anthony repeated the song that Strega Nona sang? Or might it backfire somehow? Write about what might have happened.

Fall Fever, Winter Fever, Summer Fever

Children write about and describe someone who has caught a seasonal "fever." Have them describe a person's changed behaviors and what they think caused the person to have the particular "fever."

RESPONDING TO THE TEXT: DRAMA AND MOVEMENT

Special Person Day

Using children's ideas about someone they would like to be for a day (see A Daily Schedule in the Writing response section), invite children to come to school dressed as that person. Or invite them to bring in clothing and props and give a short presentation to the class about what it might be like to be their special person.

Create a Play with Puppets

Have a committee of children put on a puppet play about *Big Anthony and the Magic Ring*. See ideas listed previously in the Drama and Art response sections for *Strega Nona* and in the Art section for this unit.

Learn How to Dance the Tarantella

Invite a dance or movement instructor to teach your children how to dance the tarantella. Bring in the appropriate music for dance practice throughout the unit. Learning about the music and dance will help children when they present the puppet play since it can provide background during their play or readers theatre presentations.

RESPONDING TO THE TEXT: ART

Add Scenes to the *Strega Nona* Mural

Using the mural and puppet activities described in the Drama and Art response sections for *Strega Nona,* have children create for the mural additional scenes that are more specific to *Big Anthony and the Magic Ring*. The village square where Big Anthony and Strega Nona dance all night is critical to the setting, so encourage children to include it on their mural.

Make Puppets for *Big Anthony and the Magic Ring*

See the Art response section in *Strega Nona* for ideas on puppet making. A group or committee of children could make puppets specific to this story while other children work on puppets for the remaining *Strega Nona* stories.

Create Magic Rings

Children create their own magic rings to wear using inexpensive plastic rings bought at a grocery or party store as the base. Invite children to bring in buttons, beads, sequins, fake jewels, and feathers to add to the rings. When enough materials are collected, have children draw up a model for their ring before creating it. You might have them describe the art materials they want to use and what each added item will do when attached to the ring base. For instance, they can draw their simple ring and label it as in the illustration below.

With some Tacky glue or a glue gun (with adult assistance), give children time to create their own special magic ring. Be sure to give children time to share with each other their magic rings, the song or chant they created, and what they hope will happen when the ring does its magic.

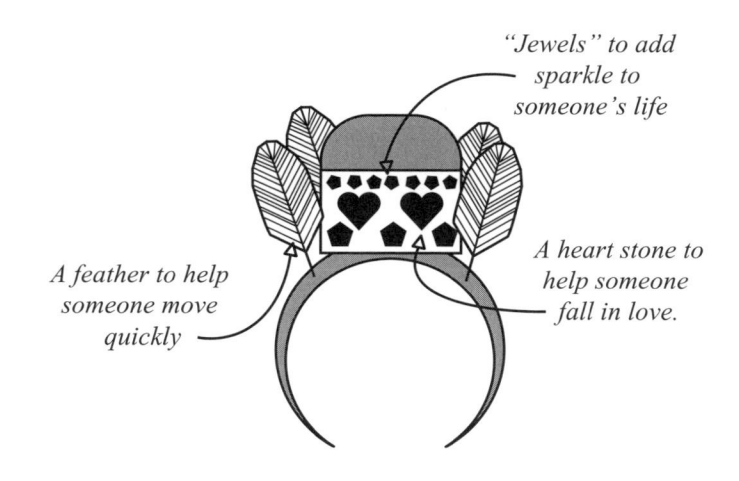

"Jewels" to add sparkle to someone's life

A feather to help someone move quickly

A heart stone to help someone fall in love.

48 ♥ On the Wing of a Whitebird

RESPONDING TO THE TEXT: SCIENCE

Other Uses for Olive Oil

Strega Nona used this classic ingredient in Italian cooking to remove a ring from Big Anthony's finger. What other uses can children think of for olive oil?

Tasting Different Oils

If you can share food in your classroom, bring in a variety of olive oils—flavored and unflavored—and have children sample them by dipping pieces of Italian bread (of course!) into them. Have them vote for their favorites and describe the differences.

Strega Nona's Magic Lessons

SUMMARY

Bambolona, the baker's daughter, is tired of working for her father. He expects her to do all of the baking while he goes off each day to visit with his friends in the square. Bambolona goes to see Strega Nona to get help in changing "the ways things are." Strega Nona suggests that Bambolona come work for her and also learn her magic. Big Anthony overhears the conversation and tells Strega Nona that he, too, wants to learn her magic. When Strega Nona tells him that she can't teach him, Big Anthony becomes angry and goes to work for Bambolona's father. He quickly bungles up things for the baker and after being fired, tells a woman in the square that if only Strega Nona had taught him to be a *Strega* he never would have left her house. When the woman asks him, "Whoever heard of a man being a Strega!?" Big Anthony gets an idea. The next thing we know, "Antonia" (Big Anthony in disguise) is knocking at Strega Nona's door just as Strega Nona is beginning a magic lesson with Bambolona. Antonia tells Strega Nona, "All my life I've wanted to learn your magic. Will you teach me? Please?" Antonia is taken in and begins to learn Strega Nona's magic right alongside Bambolona. Somehow though, Antonia never gets it quite right. One day, Antonia tries to do some *real* magic. Read with your students how Big Anthony learns the hard way that "magic can't be fooled with."

PRE-READING ACTIVITIES

Gather your children together and discuss:

- Do you remember a time when you really didn't feel appreciated? When was it? What did you do? Did you tell someone? Did you act out? What were the circumstances?

Anticipation Guide

Have your children fill out an anticipation guide, filling in their opinions to the questions in the guide. After filling these out, children can share their results with others before reading the story. You may want to have younger children respond orally.

Strega Nona's Magic Lessons Anticipation Guide

Name _____ Date _____

AGREE   **DISAGREE**

_____   _____   It's good to become angry sometimes.

_____   _____   You should always follow directions.

_____   _____   It's alright to occasionally pretend you are someone else.

Strega Nona's Magic Lessons Anticipation Guide

Name _____ Date _____

AGREE   **DISAGREE**

_____   _____   It's good to become angry sometimes.

_____   _____   You should always follow directions.

_____   _____   It's alright to occasionally pretend you are someone else.

MAKING PREDICTIONS

Show both the front and back covers of *Strega Nona's Magic Lessons* to your class and discuss:

- Do you remember the names of the characters that appear on the cover? What do you know about these characters?
- What kind of magic lessons do you think Strega Nona might be giving?
- In the last book we read about Big Anthony and Bambolona (*Big Anthony and the Magic Ring*), Bambolona seemed to take a liking to Big Anthony. What do you predict will happen to Bambolona and Big Anthony in this story?
- Is the setting the same as in the other *Strega Nona* books we have read in the past? How can you tell?

READING THE STORY

Read and enjoy *Strega Nona's Magic Lessons* with your children.

Predicting within the Story

You may want to stop at the point in the story where Big Anthony has been discovered by Bambolona. Sobbing and putting his hand over his heart, he says, "I promise, I *really* promise, that as long as I live I will never play with magic again. Just please bring Strega Nona back."

- What do you think will happen next?
- Will Strega Nona return? If so, in what form?
- What will happen to Big Anthony?

THINKING CRITICALLY ABOUT THE TEXT

- Why is Bambolona feeling unappreciated by her father?
- How do you think Bambolona expects Strega Nona to help her? Do you think she is interested in working for Strega Nona all along?
- Why do you think Strega Nona replies that she can't teach Big Anthony her magic?
- Why doesn't the bakery job work out for Big Anthony?
- Do you think Big Anthony is clever to dress up as Antonia?
- When do you think Strega Nona and Bambolona know that Antonia is really Big Anthony?
- Do you think Big Anthony is set up by Strega Nona? That Strega Nona uses the story about the special book to lure Big Anthony into wanting to surprise her but really goof up?
- What about the toad? Where does it come from?
- Can we add any descriptions to our lists that describe Strega Nona, Big Anthony, and

Bambolona? What words would you add based on our reading the story of *Strega Nona's Magic Lessons*?

SHARING PERSONAL EXPERIENCES

Give children the opportunity to respond to the following questions:

- What do you do when you are angry and are not feeling appreciated?
- What helps you control your anger?
- What do you do or who do you talk to?

RESPONDING TO THE TEXT: INTEGRATED LANGUAGE ARTS

Advice Posters

If children shared different ways of managing their anger through the Sharing Personal Experience response (see above), let them create some posters to display in the classroom and around the school so all children will benefit from their shared wisdom. If children cannot think of positive ways to manage their anger, brainstorm a list of ideas together as a class. Then, have groups of children create reminder posters to display throughout the classroom.

Create a Timeline of the History of Bread

Bambolona's father worked in a bakery providing bread, one of the staples of Italian cuisine. Using information in the History, Science, Cooking, and other response sections later in this literary guide, children work in groups to learn about and then share in picture or time line form how bread has changed throughout the years.

RESPONDING TO THE TEXT: WRITING

"That's the Way Things Are"

Children write about times when they have heard a saying like Bambolona's father told her, "life is *not* fair," and what they were frustrated with.

If Only . . .

Have children brainstorm what they would like to change about their lives if they could. What would they change and why?

Helping Bambolona

What if Strega Nona didn't need any help? How do you think she might have helped Bambolona deal with her father? Create another job for Bambolona and describe how it would be better than working for her father.

RESPONDING TO THE TEXT: DRAMA

Create a Puppet Play

Have a committee of children put on a puppet play specific to *Strega Nona's Magic Lessons*. See ideas listed previously in the Drama and Art response sections for *Strega Nona* and those included in the Art response section for this literary guide.

Playing "Dress Up"

Have children role-play some of the parts and dress up as Strega Nona, Bambolona, and Big Anthony/Antonia. Bring in simple props such as scarves and aprons and let the class have fun. Children can also practice using the "Antonia" voice Big Anthony must have used.

RESPONDING TO THE TEXT: ART

Add Scenes to the *Strega Nona* Mural

Using the mural and puppet activities described in the Drama and Art response sections for *Strega Nona*, have children create additional scenes for the mural that are more specific to *Strega Nona's Magic Lessons*. The bakery that belongs to Bambolona's father and the inside of Strega Nona's house are settings specific to the story that your committee could include on the mural.

Make Puppets for *Strega Nona's Magic Lessons*

See the Art response section in *Strega Nona* for ideas on puppet making. A group or committee of children could make puppets specific to this story while other children work on puppets for other *Strega Nona* stories.

Create a Big Anthony/Antonia Mask

Using a thick paper plate, yarn for hair, and drawing tools, children can create a two-sided mask of Big Anthony on one side and Antonia on the other side. Attach the masks to some long paint stirrers or rulers and children are ready to act out parts of the story or read parts in a readers theatre production of the story. For really intricate but fun paper masks, use ideas from the book *Paper Masks and Puppets for Stories, Sons, and Plays,* by Ron and Marsha Feller.

Create a Mask for Bambolona

Why might Bambolona want or need to disguise herself? What would she look like? Create a two-sided mask for her and tell why and when she might use her other self.

RESPONDING TO THE TEXT: MATH

Graph Favorite Kinds of Bread

Bambolona was always baking and delivering bread for her father. Have children brainstorm a list of different types of sandwich breads and then graph their favorites. It might look something like the one on the next page.

What is your favorite kind of sandwich bread?

White	Wheat	Rye	Whole grain	Other

RESPONDING TO THE TEXT: COOKING AND RELATED ACTIVITIES

Baking Bread

Baking bread takes a lot of work and a lot of time. Just ask Bambolona. Bake bread with your children, if you can, and have them experience the process and all of the steps involved. You will find step-by-step recipes in many children's cookbooks.

Invite Bakers to Speak to Your Children

Invite local bakers to your classroom to share information about their jobs and businesses. They can also explain how their particular bread is made. The children will learn a lot and hopefully have a chance to sample different types of bread.

Tour a Bread Factory

Many bread factories give tours that never cease to amaze me. Arrange a tour for your children and enjoy learning about bread production from a factory.

Watch a Video about How Bread Is Made

An excellent resource on how bread is made is the video *Bread Comes to Life: A Garden of Wheat and a Loaf to Eat*. The video is narrated by Lily Tomlin with music by George Winston. For more information about bread, including classroom activities and recipes, go to the Web site www.breadcomestolife.com.

RESPONDING TO THE TEXT: HISTORY, SCIENCE, AND OTHER ACTIVITIES

The History of Bread

Children will enjoy learning about the history of bread and how it has changed and varied in its form throughout the years. They can learn a lot and perhaps create their own time line using the book *Loaves of Fun: A History of Bread with Activities and Recipes from around the World,* by Elizabeth H. Harbison.

How and Why Does Bread Rise?

The answer to this question and others relating to bread and the powers of yeast can also be found in *Loaves of Fun: A History of Bread with Activities and Recipes from around the World*.

Balancing Acts

Bambolona balanced loaves of bread on her head from her father's bakery each day and delivered them to customers. What can your children balance on their heads? Challenge them to think of unusual items to balance on their heads. Have them sign up and share their balancing acts with one another. Just for fun, if a bakery will donate some loaves of bread, have children try to balance them on their heads. Foccacia bread would probably be the easiest bread to balance in this way.

Balancing Acts Around the World

Many people around the world balance and carry different things on their heads. Challenge children to look through books about life in different countries or in old *National Geographic* magazines to find pictures of people carrying items on their heads. What do they learn about the people? How do we carry or move similar things in our country?

Magic Tricks

Using many of the available books for children on how to perform magic tricks, invite interested children to learn some of them and plan a magic show. Or have interested children sign up to perform a magic trick at the end of each day for a week. What a great way to end your school day! Be sure children have time to share how their magic trick works and the necessary materials needed to perform it. One of the easier magic trick books I have discovered is *The Most Excellent Book of How to Be a Magician with Easy Step-by-Step Instructions for a Brilliant Performance,* by Peter Eldin.

Merry Christmas, Strega Nona

SUMMARY

"It is the first Sunday of Advent, and everyone in the little town in Calabria was busy getting ready for Christmas." Strega Nona, too, was busy preparing everything for the Christmas Eve feast that she shared with the townspeople each year. Of course, Big Anthony, who worked for Strega Nona, was kept busier than usual at this time with the cooking and cleaning and baking that had to be done. Even Bambolona wasn't around to help because she had to return to her father's bakery to help him bake all of the special cakes and cookies requested for the holiday. As Strega Nona orders Big Anthony to do this and do that, he asks why she doesn't use her magic to help the baker with all the preparations. Strega Nona sharply answers, "Not at Christmastime!" One day Strega Nona orders Big Anthony to "run down the hill and get the baccalà—the dried codfish for the Christmas stew." He is to soak it in the tub and change the water every day so it will be soft and not too salty for the Christmas stew. Once again Big Anthony asks Strega Nona why she doesn't use her magic to help do it all. And once again, Strega Nona says, "No, no magic at Christmastime. Christmas has a magic of its own."

As Big Anthony goes into town and complains to the townspeople about being ordered around by Strega Nona, he learns a bit about how important *Natale*—Christmas—is to Strega Nona. Read with your children about the very special gift Big Anthony arranges for Strega Nona. "Christmas really does have a magic of its own!"

PRE-READING ACTIVITIES

Graphing December Celebrations

Create a simple graph and encourage children to write their names above the holidays they celebrate with their families.

Your graph might include look like this:

Holidays I celebrate

Christmas	Hanukkah	Kwanzaa	Other

Other celebrations might include Our Lady of Guadalupe, St. Nicholas Day, Easter, and so on. Be sure to include some columns on your graph in which children can fill in the name of their other celebrations.

Note: The information from the graph will help you know which children celebrate holidays and which don't. It is important for you to determine if sharing books about the holidays is going to be a problem with any of your children or their parents. Taking time to do this graph with children will also prepare them for the story, *Merry Christmas, Strega Nona,* which focuses on the holiday of Christmas, as celebrated in a village in Calabria, Italy.

In addition, throughout the rest of this literary guide, whenever I refer to holidays, I use this as a general term inclusive of all. Specific holidays are mentioned by name.

MAKING PREDICTIONS

Show both the front and the back covers of *Merry Christmas, Strega Nona* to your children and discuss:

- What are some special ways you think Strega Nona might celebrate Christmas?
- What characters do you think will be in this *Strega Nona* story?
- If someone were giving a gift to Strega Nona, what might be something special to give her?

READING THE STORY

Read and enjoy the story of *Merry Christmas, Strega Nona* with your children.

Predicting within the Story

You may want to stop at the point where Strega Nona slowly leaves the church to climb the hill to her little house and ask your students:

- Why do you think Big Anthony forgets everything again, especially when he knows how important the Christmas feast is to Strega Nona?
- What do you think might happen next?

THINKING CRITICALLY ABOUT THE TEXT

- It takes Strega Nona all of Advent (four weeks prior Christmas) to prepare her Christmas Eve feast. Why?
- Why doesn't Strega Nona want to use any of her magic for the preparations?
- Why do you think Strega Nona thinks Bambolona organized the celebration for her?
- What do you think Strega Nona means when she says, "Christmas has a magic of its own"? Do you think Christmas or some other holiday is magical?
- Can we add any more adjectives (describing words) to our lists that describe Strega Nona, Big Anthony, and Bambolona? What words would you add based on our reading the story *Merry Christmas, Strega Nona*?

SHARING PERSONAL EXPERIENCES

- Does your family take time to prepare special foods for your holiday celebrations? What do they do? Do you help in the preparations?

RESPONDING TO THE TEXT: INTEGRATED LANGUAGE ARTS

Create a Family Traditions Cookbook

Invite each child to bring in a favorite recipe unique to them. (See sample of letter sent out to parents inviting them to send in a family recipe.) It may be a favorite birthday or holiday tradition. It may be a special recipe that has been handed down throughout a child's family or simply one the whole family loves. If they copy the recipe, ask their parents to check the recipe for accuracy. If you have a willing and resourceful parent, ask him or her to type up all of the recipes and bind them into a classroom cookbook.

A Note from Mrs. Hornburg

Dear Parents,

Next week we will begin a unit of study entitled "Generations" which will involve learning more about our own family's heritage, as well as those of others. As a part of this study we will be creating a classroom "Family Traditions Cookbook." We would like each family to provide one recipe that is special to them. It may be a favorite birthday or holiday tradition. It may be a recipe that has been handed down through your family or simply one that the whole family agrees is tasty.

You might want to take time to talk with your child about some of the special recipes that are unique to your family. We invite you to choose one of them and send it in with your child before Friday, November 21st. If possible, a typed version or photocopy is ideal.
Finally, if there are any parents who would be willing to do some of the typing and layout for this project, please let me know. We hope to have the books completed by mid-December.

Thanks in advance for your assistance.

To make a cover, children can draw or paint a picture of their family celebrating together in some way. These cookbooks make a wonderful holiday gift for parents!

RESPONDING TO THE TEXT: WRITING

Making Lists

How does your family prepare for the holidays (if they celebrate)? Have children make a list of things they know their family does to prepare for the holidays. Perhaps they could create a separate list for adults and one for children.

Hanukkah Is . . . Christmas Is . . . Kwanzaa Is . . .

Have children begin a simple list of words that come to mind when they think of the holiday they celebrate. If they don't participate in a celebration at this time, children could begin their list with "Winter is . . ."

Keeping Secrets

Are there times when you kept a secret and surprised someone? What did you do and how did you keep the secret? How did the person react? Write about the surprise and describe the person's reaction.

Specific Preparations

Strega Nona has very specific jobs for Big Anthony to do "her way." Are there jobs at your house your parents want you to do in a particular or special way? Why do you think this is important to them? Make a list of the jobs you or your parents do that have to be done in a very specific manner.

My Rules and Expectations

Do you expect your friends to do some things in a particular way? For instance, are there ball games or other activities that have certain rules that have to be followed? Write about or create a list of games and activities you participate in that have to be done a specific way.

Excuses

Big Anthony tells Strega Nona that he forgot to get the things on her list because there was a visiting puppet show from Venice in the village. What are some excuses you might make? What are some activities that might cause you to forget what you were asked to do for someone?

If Only Strega Nona Would Let Me Use Her Magic

Make a list of all of the jobs Big Anthony would do by magic if Strega Nona would let him. Make a list of some of your jobs or chores that you would like to have done by magic.

58 ♥ On the Wing of a Whitebird

RESPONDING TO THE TEXT: DRAMA

Create a Puppet Play

Have a committee of children put on a puppet play specific to *Merry Christmas, Strega Nona*. See ideas listed previously in the Drama and Art response sections for *Strega Nona* and those included in the Art response section of this literary guide.

Readers Theatre or Group Presentations

Children could read books to learn about other holiday celebrations, such as Hanukkah, Kwanzaa, and the Feast of our Lady of Guadalupe (December 12). Then, give each group time to plan and share the information with others through a readers theatre (if there is a short book written about the celebration) or other kind of group presentation. Through these presentations, children can educate their peers about how people around the world celebrate during this time. One group could also research information about the winter solstice and share that with the others.

RESPONDING TO THE TEXT: ART

Add Scenes to the *Strega Nona* Mural

Using the mural and puppet activities described in the Drama and Art response sections for *Strega Nona*, have children create additional scenes for the mural that are more specific to *Merry Christmas, Strega Nona*. Children may need to think of a creative way to add snow to some of the scenes. Attaching peel-and-stick Velcro tabs to the backs of newly created snow scenes might be one way for the children to add and take away the scenes that are specific to *Merry Christmas, Strega Nona*. They may also want to add a church to the area near the convent that is on the original *Strega Nona* mural.

Make Puppets for *Merry Christmas, Strega Nona*

See the Art response section in *Strega Nona* for ideas on puppet making. A group or committee of children could make puppets specific to this story while other children work on puppets for the other *Strega Nona* stories.

Painting Family Celebrations

Provide watercolors or tempera paint for children to paint a picture of a family celebration. Have them think about the celebration and try to capture a favorite moment in time. Perhaps they could look at photos taken at past family celebrations to note some of the details to include in their paintings. These paintings could be displayed together with a short description written by each child. Or they could use the painting as a book cover. Children could write about their family celebration and bind it into a book with the painting on the cover.

Painting with a "Bird's Eye View"

In the video *A Visit with Tomie dePaola* (see Chapter 5), Tomie shows us a painting of a Mexican dinner influenced by the art of Frida Kahlo. He has painted a giant rendition of a Mexican meal, complete with plates of food and the centerpiece. Watch this part of the video, if possible, and then have children plan an oversized painting of their favorite family meal, looking at it from above as if they are in a miniature airplane flying over their family table. Encourage children to think carefully about the color of the tablecloth, food, centerpieces, candles, and other items they would find on a celebration table at their house. After they have planned their illustration, give them oversized paper to sketch again and then paint their bird's eye view of their family meal.

Note: If you give this assignment before a holiday such as Thanksgiving, children can sketch or take a picture of the dinner table before people are seated, which will assist them in their painting.

RESPONDING TO THE TEXT: COMMUNITY BUILDING

Secret Pals

Some children really enjoy choosing a "secret pal" during special times of the year. Each child chooses the name of another child in class and does secret little things for that person. This has always worked best when my class has had a long discussion about ways to do little kindnesses for one another. I have never had children spend money on each other or exchange gifts. We challenge each other to send notes, draw pictures, or be a special friend to their secret pal until the time when children get to guess who their special person is. Spending a week on this activity always seems adequate and all children have to agree to participate in it to create a positive experience for the class. Most children really love to participate in secret pal activities. You probably have your own secret pal "traditions." Share them with your children and decide together how you want to proceed.

Helping People in Need

During the holiday season there are always people or organizations in need of assistance. Help your children choose a family, group of children, or organization to assist during the holidays or other time of year. (People are not only in need during the holidays.) Young children have a hard time relating to the idea of helping others outside of their own families or immediate situations. I have found that they can relate to situations where children their age are involved. For instance, one year our school collected school supplies and books for a transitional school for homeless children. The students could, with assistance, begin to understand that there were children who don't have their own school supplies or books. The collection was quite a success and the children felt good about their efforts. You will need to decide if an activity like this is appropriate for your children, because some of you will be teaching children from families that need assistance themselves. Strega Nona was very gracious in hosting a holiday party every year for her village. Sharing her example will help children relate to the concept of giving to others.

Helping Our Wild Friends

There are many ways for children to remember the birds and animals in their area during the cold winter months. One way is to make bird feeders or edible (for birds and animals) ornaments and garlands that can be strung on outdoor trees to attract and feed animal friends. There are some great ideas and directions in the book *ECOART! Earth-Friendly Art & Craft Experiences for 3–9-year-olds,* by Laurie Carlson. You will find many ideas in other children's nature activity books.

Strega Nona Meets Her Match

SUMMARY

Strega Nona has no idea that when her good friend Strega Amelia comes to visit, she, too, will decide to set up her own business in the little town of Calabria. Strega Nona is not concerned at first about Strega Amelia's giving out *dolci*—sweets—and cappuccino to all of her customers or her use of the latest scientific equipment. Yet, one day, not one single person comes to see Strega Nona. After three weeks with no customers, she sadly has to let go of her assistants, Big Anthony and Bambolona, because without business she can no longer pay them. Bambolona returns to work at her father's bakery, but Big Anthony gets a job working for Strega Amelia. Bambolona thinks Big Anthony is a traitor, but Strega Nona wishes Big Anthony *buona fortuna*—good luck. Big Anthony does a great job for Strega Amelia, and her business is booming. One day, confident in her business and Big Anthony's assistance, Strega Amelia leaves Big Anthony in charge for a few days while she journeys over the mountain to get the rest of her equipment. Read the story with your children to find out why, when Strega Amelia returns, she is greeted by the mayor who tells her that everyone in the little town agrees they prefer the "old ways" and "our own Strega Nona is enough for us."

PRE-READING ACTIVITIES

MAKING PREDICTIONS

Show both the front and back covers of *Strega Nona Meets Her Match* to your class and discuss:

- Who do you think the other woman is on the front cover?
- How does she look different from Strega Nona? How does she look the same?
- What does it mean to "meet your match"?
- What do you think this might mean for Strega Nona?

READING THE STORY

Read and enjoy the story of *Strega Nona Meets Her Match* with your children.

Predicting within the Story

You may want to stop at the point where Strega Nona has to let go of her assistants, Big Anthony and Bambolona. Ask your children:

- What do you think will happen to Strega Nona now? What will she do?
- What might happen to Bambolona when she goes to work for her father?
- How do you think Big Anthony will do working for Strega Amelia?

THINKING CRITICALLY ABOUT THE TEXT

- Are Strega Nona and Strega Amelia good friends? Why or why not?
- Why do you think Strega Amelia decides to start a business just like Strega Nona's in the same town?

- Why do you think the townspeople decide to switch from seeing Strega Nona to Strega Amelia instead? Is it just because she is giving away free food?
- Why do you think Bambolona and Strega Nona react the way they do when they find out that Big Anthony is going to work for Strega Amelia? How can Strega Nona wish Big Anthony good luck?
- Why do you think Big Anthony does his jobs perfectly while Strega Amelia is around and makes so many mistakes when she is gone?
- Do you think Strega Amelia will ever really discover why her customers return to Strega Nona?

SHARING PERSONAL EXPERIENCES

- Have you ever had to compete with one of your best friends? What did it feel like? Was your friendship affected?

RESPONDING TO THE TEXT: INTEGRATED LANGUAGE ARTS

A Visit with Good Friends

When Strega Amelia comes to visit, she and Strega Nona talk and laugh and gossip. Write about a good friend you like to spend time with. Choose a special place you like to go or an activity you like to do together and draw a picture of you and your friend enjoying each other's company.

Create Business Cards or Handbills for Strega Amelia and Strega Nona

Strega Amelia has a handbill distributed advertising her new business. Create a business card for Strega Amelia or a handbill or business card for Strega Nona. How will the advertising for Strega Nona and Strega Amelia differ but still attract business?

Create Your Own *Strega* or *Stregone* (Male *Strega*) Business

Children create their own business by deciding on a special skill they can share with others. Have children decide what kind of advertising they are going to use to bring in business. Give them time to create their own handbill, business card, or advertisements and share them with each another.

RESPONDING TO THE TEXT: WRITING

Dear *Stregas*—Point of View

Bring in some Dear Abby columns (choose appropriate ones) from your local newspaper (or a similar type column) and share the format with your children. Have children write a letter to Strega Nona and Strega Amelia asking for advice in solving some kind of problem. Then, divide up the letters among your children, making sure each child doesn't get his or her own letter requesting help. Have children answer the letters first from Strega Nona's point of view and then from Strega Amelia's.

How will the answers differ? Children may find it easier to pair up and collaborate on answering the letters. Give plenty of time for children to share the letters and their answers. If possible, display them for all to enjoy.

Dear Strega Amelia . . .

Write a letter to Strega Amelia from Strega Nona. What might it say? Tell how Strega Nona's business has been affected by Strega Amelia's. Or is the letter written after Strega Amelia's return to her own town because Big Anthony bungled up her business?

Free Giveaways

Don't you love it when stores give out free items or food just for coming into the store? Have you ever gone to a grand opening because they were giving things away? Write about where you went and what you received. Was the store honest in telling what it was going to give away or was the ad exaggerated?

RESPONDING TO THE TEXT: DRAMA

Create a Puppet Play

Have a committee of children put on a puppet play specific to *Strega Nona Meets Her Match*. See ideas listed previously in the Drama and Art response sections for *Strega Nona* and those in the Art response section for this literary guide.

Role-Playing *Stregas* and *Stregone*

If children created their own *Strega* characters in the above Integrated Language Arts response section, have them create their own costume or clothing and act out the role. Perhaps they can convince another child to act as someone in need and role-play how they would help that person.

RESPONDING TO THE TEXT: ART

Add Scenes to the *Strega Nona* Mural

Using the mural and puppet activities described in the Drama and Art response sections for *Strega Nona,* have children create additional scenes for the mural that are more specific to *Strega Nona Meets Her Match*. Children will want to add a house for Strega Amelia. They may also want to depict the inside of her house with its modern technology and machinery.

Make Puppets for *Strega Nona Meets Her Match*

See the Art response section in *Strega Nona* for ideas on making puppets. A group or committee of children could make puppets specific to this story while other children work on puppets for the other *Strega Nona* stories. The character of Strega Amelia will need to be added to this story.

♥♥♥ — ♥♥♥ — ♥♥♥ — ♥♥♥ — ♥♥♥ — ♥♥♥

Big Anthony's "Healing" Ways

People come to Big Anthony with a problem.

Big Anthony's solution is in progress.

Big Anthony's solution backfires.

♥♥♥ — ♥♥♥ — ♥♥♥ — ♥♥♥ — ♥♥♥ — ♥♥♥

Create a Magical Hat

Using an old hat as a base, add feathers, sequins, and trim to make a hat like Strega Amelia's. Children can wear their hats while answering letters in the activity listed above to Strega Nona and Strega Amelia or while dressing up as a *Strega* or *Stregone*.

Big Anthony's "Healing" Ways

Find the two pages in the book where Tomie dePaola illustrates Big Anthony running the husband-and-wife machine backwards and confuses the wart cream with the hair remover. Tomie has used a specific format on these two pages. Using the form that follows, have children draw people coming to Big Anthony with a problem in the top rectangle, his solution in progress in the middle two boxes, and then the problem being bungled in the bottom two boxes.

Home Interiors

Using *Strega Nona Meets Her Match* and some of the previous *Strega Nona* books, have children research and then draw the interiors of both Strega Nona's and Strega Amelia's homes. They might want to focus on the rooms where the people come to be "cured." If children create their own *Strega* or *Stregone* characters, they can draw the interior of the "their" home.

RESPONDING TO THE TEXT: SCIENCE

What Would Happen If?

We all know that adding a little baking soda to a jar of vinegar will cause a chemical reaction. Explore this and other simple science or cooking experiments. There may be some in the textbooks or science trade books you have around. Ask children to predict what would happen if you added too much of one ingredient (like baking powder or yeast) to a recipe or experiment. Would it turn out the same? Children will be able to relate to the mistakes that Big Anthony makes when mixing up ingredients.

Performing Science Experiments and Tricks

Children love to rehearse and perform science tricks and experiments for one another. Provide some of the *Bet You Can* series of paperback science experiment books for children by Vicki Cobb and Kathy Darling. Give children time to choose and rehearse the experiment or trick of their choice and then share it with the rest of the class. Titles in the series include *Bet You Can! Science Possibilities to Fool You*, *Bet You Can't: Science Impossibilities to Fool You*, and *Wanna Bet?: Science Challenges to Fool You*.

Design a Machine for Strega Amelia

Children may want to create their own machines that cure headaches and other ailments. Using cardboard tubes, boxes, and art materials, have children work in groups to create a headache machine or other helpful machine. Be sure they have time to paint them and then label and describe what each part of the machine does. If children really get excited about their machine, they can create a handbill or poster advertising the machine's amazing feats. For other design ideas for children, consult the book *Design Technology: Children's Engineering,* by Susan Dunn and Rob Larson.

Strega Nona: Her Story

SUMMARY

Strega Nona: Her Story is the prequel to the *Strega Nona* series of books by Tomie dePaola. The story takes place in the town of Calabria in southern Italy on a cold and blustery night. A young mother is having difficulty giving birth to her child. Grandma Concetta arrives on the scene, assists in bringing little Nona into the world, and declares that she will grow up to be a *Strega*. The story follows Nona as she learns the ways of Grandma Concetta and makes fast friends with Amelia, her classmate, and it explains how Nona and Amelia's paths change when they go off to study at the Accademia delle Streghe.

Nona misses the old ways of Grandma Concetta so much that she leaves Amelia to study at the Academia and returns home. Saddened that she will never receive an official *"Strega"* diploma, Nona is comforted by Grandma Concetta when she says, "you don't need a diploma to be a true Strega. You already have everything you need. You have the spirit and kindness that come from the heart. And when I pass my practice over to you, I will tell you the *ingrediente segreto*—the secret ingredient. Then you will be not only a true Strega, but a great one."

Grandma Concetta grows old and passes her practice over to Nona, who is then "officially" called Strega Nona. Read with your children to learn about the secret ingredient that Nona discovers.

PRE-READING ACTIVITIES

Sharing a Prequel

Since this is the prequel to the *Strega Nona* stories, some people may think that beginning with *Strega Nona: Her Story* would be a good way to begin a unit of all of the stories by Tomie dePaola. However, to prepare your children for *Strega Nona: Her Story,* it is actually best if they have already experienced the original story of *Strega Nona* and some of its characters in their original setting.

Read the original *Strega Nona* story with your children or watch the video of the story available from Children's Circle. When children know who Big Anthony, Bambolona, and Amelia are, they will enjoy reading about Strega Nona's past.

What Is a Biographer? A Portraitist?

Gather your children together and discuss:

- Do you know what a biographer is? Tomie dePaola is the biographer for Strega Nona, which means he writes the story of her life. She "tells" Tomie how to write and tell the stories about her early life. Have you read or heard any other biographies?
- Have you ever heard of someone creating a portrait? Tomie is also Strega Nona's portraitist. What do you think that might mean?

Give children time to share if their families have any written diaries or biographies of older family members or ancestors. Also have them share times they may have participated in family portraits being taken. What was that like? Ask them why they think families go to all the trouble of having family portraits taken?

MAKING PREDICTIONS

As you gather the children together around you with a copy of *Strega Nona: Her Story,* discuss:

- What do you notice about the cover?
- Where do you think the story takes place? (the setting)
- Who do you think is in the picture frame?

READING THE STORY

This is a great opportunity to share various parts of a book with your children.

Inside front flap

- Let's read the flap on the inside front cover of the book before we begin the story. It really is the beginning of the story.

Title page

- Next notice the title page. Here is a picture of Tomie taking down notes from Strega Nona or acting as a biographer. What else do you notice?

Dedication page

- Have you ever seen a picture of a stork delivering a child like this? Tomie's love of white doves shows in his version of the delivery of a new child. What do we learn from Tomie dePaola's dedication?

Predicting within the Story

- You might want to stop at the point where Grandma Concetta is consoling Nona about studying with her instead of going to the Accademia delle Streghe. When she talks about the *ingrediente segreto,* you could have your children write down their predictions about what they think the secret ingredient might be.

THINKING CRITICALLY ABOUT THE TEXT

- Where does the story take place?
- Can you find the area of Calabria on a map of Italy?
- What are some of the early lessons Nona learned from Grandma Concetta?
- How were young Nona and Amelia alike? Different?
- Nona and Amelia studied to be *Stregas* in two different ways. Do you think one way is better than the other? Why or why not?
- Tomie dePaola uses interesting borders for many of his pictures. What is he sharing through these borders?
- Why do you think Grandma Concetta waited until she retired to share with Nona the secret ingredient?

Venn Diagram
Comparing Nona and Amelia

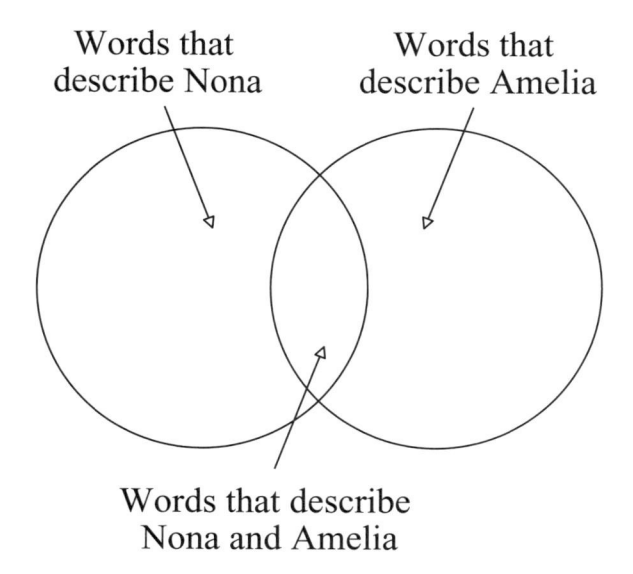

Words that describe Nona

Words that describe Amelia

Words that describe Nona and Amelia

RESPONDING TO THE TEXT: INTEGRATED LANGUAGE ARTS

Comparing Nona and Amelia

Create a Venn diagram listing the similarities and differences between Nona and Amelia. Children can compare information shared through both the text and through Tomie dePaola's illustrations.

Note: For younger children or as an alternative to using a Venn diagram on the board or on chart paper, bring in two hula hoops and use note cards for writing characteristics describing Nona and Amelia. Overlap the hula hoops to create a Venn diagram, label the sections "Nona" and "Amelia" with folded propped-up note cards, and have children place the appropriate characteristics in each section of the Venn. This is a much more concrete way to introduce comparison to children.

Time Line Accordion Books

Younger children can illustrate and older children can write and illustrate time line books that document their growth as children. Prior to this activity, ask parents to assist you by filling in a quick form that tells one significant event for each year of their child's life. Return to *Strega Nona: Her Story* to revisit how Tomie dePaola illustrates Nona's growth over time in the circular pictures at the top of several pages. Have children choose one event to highlight and draw from each year of their lives. Decide on the size of paper to use and the art medium (e.g., paint, colored pencil, crayon, watercolors). Give children time to create a picture for each year of their lives. Some of these pictures may need to be created at home if you are short on time. Or the job can be set up at an art center for children to visit throughout each day.

When the illustrations are done, have children (or adult volunteers) create accordion books by folding colored butcher paper into sections that accommodate the size of the drawings or paintings completed. Then, with assistance, guide children in gluing and placing their completed illustrations on the accordion-folded paper. Children can write their own captions or dictate them to an adult for each picture

Text   Illustration

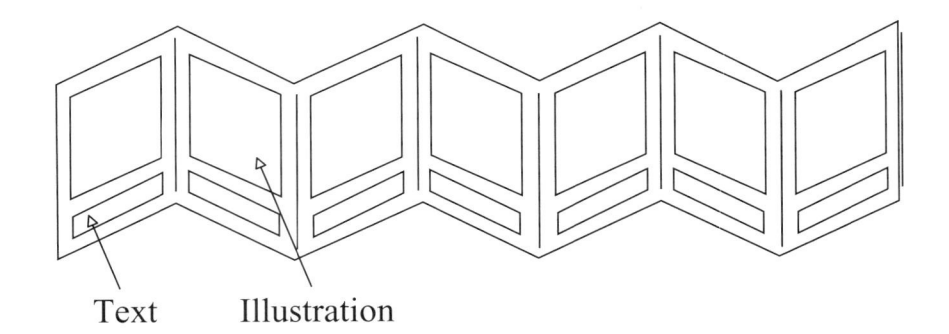

in their book. Together as a class, decide how to create a special cover for the books and tie them together with beautiful ribbons or yarn.

Easier Time Lines

Younger children can illustrate and older children can write and illustrate their autobiographies using time lines to assist them. Explain the difference between biographies and autobiographies to your children. Then demonstrate how to draw a time line and label it for each year of their life. Have children create one illustration for each year of their lives (see illustration below). Older children can go on to write a short story or paragraph for each year of their lives, edit them with assistance, and then bind them.

On the Day I was Born Collage

Strega Nona: Her Story begins with Strega Nona's birth. Have children ask their parents and grandparents about the day they were born. Some parents will have saved the newspaper or other artifacts from the day and time their child was born. Let children write descriptions from the information they gather and then perhaps work with their parents or other adults to create a collage on tag board or railroad board about the day they were born. You may choose to bind these into books instead.

Examples of what children might bring in

- a photocopy of a birth certificate or of their footprints taken at birth
- information about their height and weight
- cards received on the day of their birth
- written reflections from their grandparents or anyone else who celebrated their birth
- photos from their birth or time shortly thereafter

Timeline

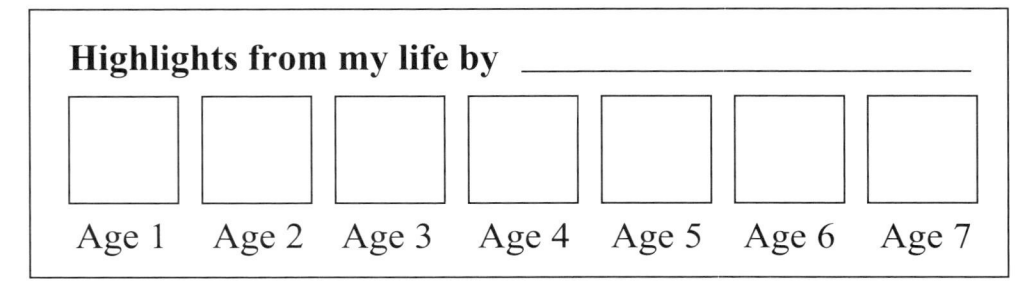

Highlights from my life by _____

| Age 1 | Age 2 | Age 3 | Age 4 | Age 5 | Age 6 | Age 7 |

RESPONDING TO THE TEXT: WRITING

Career Day or Writing Biographies

If you have a school career day, children interview someone in a career they are interested in and write a biography about that person. Or children can simply learn about and interview someone they look up to and write and then share their stories with one another. You might suggest that they use a tape recorder in collecting their information.

Strega Leah, Strega Antonia, Stregone John . . .

Children create their own *Strega* characters, stories, and the cures that help the people in their world. They might want to borrow the first names of their grandparents or important people in their lives.

Sing a New Song

Children create new songs or chants for Strega Nona. First, have them decide what Strega Nona might need a song for. Then, in groups, create a new song to some familiar tune like "Row, Row, Row Your Boat" or "Are You Sleeping?" Give them time to share their songs with the rest of the class.

RESPONDING TO THE TEXT: DRAMA

Create a Puppet Play

Have a committee of children put on a puppet play specific to *Strega Nona: Her Story*. See ideas listed previously in the Drama and Art response sections for *Strega Nona* and in the Art response section for this literary guide.

Role-Playing

Children might enjoy acting out the story of Strega Nona's life or parts of it. There are some really funny events in the story, but children also like to make up their own events. See what fun they have when they create their own adventures for Strega Nona and Strega Amelia!

RESPONDING TO THE TEXT: ART

Add Scenes to the *Strega Nona* Mural

Using the mural and puppet activities described in the Drama and Art response sections for *Strega Nona,* have children create additional scenes for the mural that are more specific to *Strega Nona: Her Story*. The Accademia delle Streghe will need to be added.

Make Puppets for *Strega Nona: Her Story*

See the Art response section in *Strega Nona* for ideas on puppet making. A group or committee of children could make puppets specific to this story while other children work on puppets for the remaining *Strega Nona* stories.

Portraits

Children can create self-portraits or portraits of other people in their lives to share.

Before and After... Cures!

Children create their own problems and cures for villagers who come to see Strega Nona. They can artistically depict what the villagers looked like before and after Strega Nona's help. Some ideas you might want to try:

Paper plate characters

- For an ailment that involves the face or head—on one paper plate have children draw or paint the villager with the problem. On another paper plate, create the villager after Strega Nona cures him or her. Insert a ruler in between the two paper plates and staple the outside edges so they can be flipped back and forth or hang them by string so they rotate around.

Pop-ups

- On the outside of a card, have children draw the villager with the problem and on the inside a pop-up character of how they look after Strega Nona magically cures them.

Before and after ads

- Children create some advertisements for Strega Nona. They can create before and after posters encouraging people to come to Strega Nona for help.

RESPONDING TO THE TEXT: SCIENCE

Learn about Healing Herbs

Grandma Concetta teaches Nona how to use many herbs for medicinal purposes. Teach your class about some herbs that are commonly used by people today for their ailments. You could grow some of the following herbs in the classroom or in a schoolyard garden:

- Echinecea (purple cone flower). When the root of this purple cone flower is boiled for tea, it is supposed to build your immune system and help get rid of colds.
- Mother of thyme. A tea compress made from this herb is supposed to help soothe scrapes and bruises.
- Chamomile. This tea is supposed to settle your stomach if you have eaten too much of something, like too many sweets! Remember, Peter Rabbit's mother gave him chamomile tea when Peter ate too much from Farmer MacGregor's garden.
- Aloe. This plant has long been known for its leaves, which contain a gel-like substance that helps soothe sunburn and minor burns.
- Mint. This tea is also supposed to aid digestion if you have eaten very spicy food or have eaten too much. Mint is very easy to grow and children can plant the herbs and then transfer them to little planters as a Mother's Day or other gift.

Children could make up names for the teas that are made from some of the herbs. As an example, you can show the children a box of Sleepytime Tea from Celestial Seasonings, which is made of several herbs.

Have an Herbal Tea Party

Let children taste some of the more common herbal teas. Have them vote on their favorites.

Teas for Kids!

Children can create a list of teas that they think companies should make just for kids. Possibilities might be pre-soccer-energy tea and help-me-focus-on-my-piano-lesson tea.

There are many more herbs and their medicinal uses you can research with your children. The ideas above come from the book *Kids Garden! The Anytime, Anyplace Guide to Sowing & Growing Fun,* by Avery Hart and Paul Mantell.

Big Anthony: His Story

SUMMARY

This book is a biography about Big Anthony, Strega Nona's lovable and very distractible assistant. In a similar format to the book *Strega Nona: Her Story,* Tomie dePaola acts as biographer and portraitist for Big Anthony.

Tomie dePaola begins by telling us of Anthony's birth on an Italian farm. Even at his christening, Nonna Graziella, Anthony's grandmother, notices that Anthony might be a "little different." We see through illustrations and the telling of the story how easily distracted Anthony is, even as a young boy. He grows so very tall that everyone begins to call him "Big Anthony." As a student and as a helper on his family farm, his short attention span becomes very clear. His teachers keep on saying, "*Attenzione, Anthony—per favore*—please pay attention!" He bumbles up so many things at school and on the family farm that finally, his family sends him out in the world before he ruins their entire fortune.

Anthony proceeds to travel through Italy, humorously leaving his mark on the famous and familiar cities of Firenze (Florence), Roma (Rome), Pisa, and Napoli (Naples). Anthony eventually heads south to Calabria, where he sees a sign in the square stating that someone on the hill needs a helper. A simple knock on the door and, as Tomie dePaola writes, "the rest is history."

Prior to Reading *Big Anthony: His Story*

I highly encourage you to read the original version of *Strega Nona* prior to reading *Big Anthony: His Story*. It helps if children already know that Big Anthony is easily distracted and messes up most directions he is given. *Big Anthony: His Story* ends with a knock on the door that is so familiar to us from the first story of *Strega Nona*.

PRE-READING ACTIVITIES

These suggestions are similar to those shared in the *Strega Nona: Her Story* literary guide. They are shared again here, for those who may have not shared that book prior to reading *Big Anthony: His Story* to students.

- Do you know what a *biographer* is? Tomie dePaola is the biographer for Big Anthony, which means he writes the story of his life. Have you read or heard any biographies before?

MAKING PREDICTIONS

Show the front cover of *Big Anthony: His Story* to your students and ask:

- What do you notice about the cover?
- Can you predict the setting for this story?
- Can you predict some events in Big Anthony's life?

THINKING CRITICALLY ABOUT THE TEXT

- Why does Anthony's Grandma, Nonna Graziella, have doubts about Anthony being a "good bambino," even at his christening?
- What are some of the ways Anthony becomes distracted as a boy? As an adult?
- Tomie dePaola doesn't always use writing to tell parts of this story. Find in the text where the pictures tell the story.
- How does Big Anthony "leave his mark" on places in Firenze, Roma, Napoli, and Pisa? What goes wrong?
- When Mt. Vesuvius begins to erupt, why do you think Big Anthony says, "at least that's not my fault."
- Looking at the back cover of the book, what do you see happening? How is this similar or different than illustrations in *Strega Nona: Her Story*?

SHARING PERSONAL EXPERIENCES

Personal Distractions

What distracts you when you are trying to focus? Music? Animals barking? Birds singing? People talking loudly? Talk about things that distract you during classroom sharing time.

RESPONDING TO THE TEXT: INTEGRATED LANGUAGE ARTS

Classroom Distractions

Use the activity above (Personal Distractions) to introduce the classroom topic of "Distractions: things that distract us when we are working." Encourage all children to share at least one thing that causes them to lose their focus when they are trying to work in the classroom. When everyone has shared, list the top five classroom distractions. Divide the classroom into committees to create decorative posters encouraging all in the classroom to respect other's study needs. An example of a poster might look like the sample shown on p. 73.

Oh No, Not *That* Big Anthony!

Tomie dePaola illustrates how the farmyard looks after Big Anthony leaves the gates open. Encourage children to think of another mistake Big Anthony might have made while helping at school or on the family farm. Provide art materials for them to share the mistake.

Please do NOT sharpen pencils during quiet time!

RESPONDING TO THE TEXT: WRITING

Memory Tricks

Big Anthony could use some help in remembering to follow through on tasks. Create a list of ideas that might help him remember directions correctly. For example, perhaps you might recommend that he make a list of things he is asked to do.

A Note to Strega Nona—A Reference Letter

Usually when you apply for a job an employer asks for letters of reference from people you have worked for in the past. What would a reference letter for Big Anthony look and sound like? Write a letter from the point of view of one of his teachers, a restaurant owner, the Roma bridge tender, or someone you think Anthony may have worked for. Is there anything positive you could say about Big Anthony?

Applying for a Job

Using the book as reference, list all of the jobs Big Anthony tries. How would these look on a résumé?

Odd Jobs

When Anthony leaves his family farm, he isn't trained in a particular trade or career so he takes odd jobs, doing work to make money to live on. He tries to mix paint, collect bridge tolls, and work in a restaurant. What kind of odd jobs can you think of that you might be interested in doing to earn some money? Or what kind of career would you like to work in when you grow up?

A Different Ending

Give the story a different ending. What if Strega Nona was not home the day Big Anthony knocks on the door? What do you think would happen? Would Big Anthony wait? Would he go to some other house on the hill? Write a new ending and share it with your classmates.

RESPONDING TO THE TEXT: ART

Add Scenes to the *Strega Nona* Mural

Using the mural and puppet activities described in the Drama and Art response sections of *Strega Nona*, have children create additional scenes for the mural that are more specific to *Big Anthony: His Story*. I encourage you to have children add the Leaning Tower of Pisa and buildings from Firenze and Roma. If you still have room, you might add Anthony's family farm.

Make Puppets for *Big Anthony: His Story*

See the Art response section in *Strega Nona* for ideas on puppet making. A group or committee of children could make puppets specific to this story while other children work on puppets for the remaining *Strega Nona* stories. You might add Anthony's parents, teachers, and grandmother.

RESPONDING TO THE TEXT: GEOGRAPHY

Using a map and a photo travel guidebook of Italy, find the following places depicted in *Big Anthony: His Story*:

- Pisa and the Leaning Tower of Pisa
- Firenze (Florence) and the Duomo
- Roma (Rome), the Coliseum, and the Vatican
- Napoli (Naples)
- Calabria. If you have shared previous *Strega Nona* books with your children, they may already know where Calabria is.

Strega Nona Takes a Vacation

SUMMARY

Strega Nona hasn't taken a vacation in the longest time. In a dream, she envisions herself playing at Grandma Concetta's house at the beach. Since Grandma Concetta has been gone for many years, Strega Nona is confused about the meaning of the dream until in another dream, Grandma tells her that "you've been working so hard all these years. You must take *una vacanza*—a vacation. Bambolona can do the daily remedies and Big Anthony can look after the house and garden."

So off Strega Nona goes to Grandma's house at the seashore, promising that she will be in touch with Bambolona and Big Anthony. She rests, swims, collects shells, cooks, and unwinds—the vacation is very good for her. She sends presents to Big Anthony and Bambolona—seashore candy for Big Anthony and bubble bath for Bambolona. Bambolona opens the presents first and sees the tags indicating who each gift is for. She decides that *she* wants the candy and switches the tags. Who could guess how much could go wrong with the simple switching of a tag?

PRE-READING ACTIVITIES

Gather your children together and discuss:

- What are several reasons people choose to take vacations? Have children share with one another the reasons they know their parents choose to take vacations with or without them.

MAKING PREDICTIONS

As you gather the children together around you with a copy of *Strega Nona Takes a Vacation,* discuss:

- Why do you think Strega Nona needs to take a vacation?
- Looking at the cover of the book, where does it appear Strega Nona goes on vacation?
- Finding Calabria on the map. Can you tell where the seashore might be that Strega Nona goes to for vacation? Try to locate several possibilities.
- What do you think someone like Strega Nona might like to do to relax and unwind?

READING THE STORY

Read and enjoy the story of *Strega Nona Takes a Vacation* with your students.

THINKING CRITICALLY ABOUT THE TEXT

- Strega Nona has a very real dream about Grandma Concetta. Why can't she get the dream out of her mind?
- How can Big Anthony, Bambolona, and the villagers tell that Strega Nona is distracted?
- Why hasn't Strega Nona taken a vacation for so long?
- Why is she able to go on vacation now?
- What are all of the ways Strega Nona relaxes at the seashore?
- Why does she swim with so many clothes on?
- It is not like Bambolona to do something wrong, like switching the tags on packages. Why do you think she does it now?
- Is the overflowing of the bubble bath really Big Anthony's fault?
- Do you think Bambolona learns her lesson?

RESPONDING TO THE TEXT: INTEGRATED LANGUAGE ARTS

Dreams

Have you ever had any vivid dreams that you still remember? If so, draw a picture and write a short description of it. Was it a scary, silly, or fun dream? Would you like to have that dream again?

Interview Others about Dreams

Some people love to talk about their dreams and even record them after they have had them. Talk to friends or family and ask them to share any dreams they especially remember. Did anyone's dream ever come true?

RESPONDING TO THE TEXT: WRITING

Temptations #1

Have you ever been tempted to do something, like switch tags on presents? If you have, write about the incident if you can. If you haven't, what kind of situation would tempt you to do something like what Bambolona does?

Temptations #2

Bambolona is tempted by the seashore candy. What are some of your temptations? Make a list of at least five things you love that might tempt you to act different than usual.

My Ideal Vacation

Brainstorm a list of at least six places you would like to go on vacation. Share the list with a friend. Are any of your ideal vacation spots the same?

RESPONDING TO THE TEXT: ART

My Ideal Vacation, Revisited

Using the list created in the previous section (My Ideal Vacation), choose one ideal vacation spot. Now, divide a large piece of poster-sized paper into four sections. Draw at least four activities you would participate in if you went on your ideal vacation. For instance, if you went to Disneyland, you might ride a roller coaster, go on smaller rides, eat dinner, or get characters' signatures.

Travel Poster Critique

Could your poster above be used as an ad for a travel agency? Post the ideal vacation posters on bulletin boards or a wall for all children to see. Have a discussion about which places all children would like to visit, which places some have already visited, or other ideas that come to mind for vacations.

Create Gift Tags

Using leftover scraps of paper, create little designs to be glued onto the scraps to make gift tags. Don't forget to add a little tie at one end, or punch a hole into it with a three-hole punch so it can be attached to a package.

Add Scenes to the *Strega Nona* Mural

Using the mural and puppet activities described in the Drama and Art response sections for *Strega Nona*, have children create additional scenes for the mural that are more specific to *Strega Nona Takes a Vacation*. Add the seashore, the changing tent, and bubbles going through town. See the idea for attaching the bubbles over the pasta with Velcro in the literary guide for *Merry Christmas, Strega Nona*.

Make Puppets for *Strega Nona Takes a Vacation*

See the Art response section in *Strega Nona* for ideas on puppet making. A group or committee of children could make puppets specific to this story while other children work on puppets for the remaining *Strega Nona* stories.

Create a Puppet Play

Have a committee of children put on a puppet play specific to *Strega Nona Takes a Vacation*. See ideas listed previously in the Drama and Art response sections for *Strega Nona* and in the Art response section for this literary guide.

Role-Playing

Children might enjoy acting out the story of *Strega Nona Takes a Vacation*. If Big Anthony and Bambolona joined her sometime, how would the vacation change? Would it be as relaxing for Strega Nona? Can you picture Big Anthony and Bambolona getting ready to swim? See what fun children have when they create their own adventures for Strega Nona, Big Anthony, and Bambolona on vacation.

RESPONDING TO THE TEXT: MATH

Graph: Have You Ever Taken a Bubble Bath?

Big Anthony had never seen bubble bath before. Using a simple yes or no graph, interview children as to whether or not they have ever had a bubble bath.

Have you ever taken a bubble bath?

Yes   No

Do you prefer taking a bath or a shower?

Bath	Shower

Bath or Shower Graph

Do you prefer taking a bath (bubbles or not) or a shower?
Create a graph where each child shows his or her preference as to how they like to get clean.

RESPONDING TO THE TEXT: SCIENCE

Bubble Science

Learn about the science of bubbles by creating your own. Have contests to see who can create the largest bubbles, the smallest bubbles, or the most creative bubble wands. For more information about creating bubbles, you might look in the following resources: *The Unbelievable Bubble Book,* by John Cassidy, *Bubbles: A Children's Museum Activity Book,* by Bernie Zubrowski and Joan Drescher, and *Bubblemania,* by Penny Raife Durant.

Create Your Own Bubble Bath

Create bubble bath for yourself or perhaps your mom by using the following simple recipe taken from *Bubblemania,* by Penny Raife Durant.

Bubble Bath Bubbles

¼ cup liquid bubble bath

¼ cup water

1 Tablespoon dishwashing liquid

Put into a beautiful bottle, tie a ribbon around it, and you have an instant gift for you or a special person in your life. Don't forget the gift tag!

Read a Bubble Story

Read *The Bubble Factory,* by Tomie dePaola, for another great story about bubbles. See reference to this book and an activity in the chapter for celebrating Tomie dePaola.

Chapter 3

The Irish Stories

INTRODUCTION

I grew up believing in leprechauns, thanks to my Irish grandfather, Leroy Maher. He would sit me on his lap and tell me all about Ireland, where his grandparents came from, and have me believing in the "wee little folk" who always had a pot of gold at the end of the rainbow.

I was not surprised to read that Tomie dePaola's grandfather had also read and shared stories with him. Tomie dePaola is of Irish and Italian descent, and a lot of his stories have the flavor of Italy and the mischief (or should I say blarney) of Ireland in them. When I discovered that Tomie dePaola had written and illustrated some Irish folktales, I was immediately interested in using them in the classroom and creating another literary guide for teachers to use. I also wanted to increase my own knowledge about Ireland and Irish folktales, so I looked forward to creating fun activities to use and share with my own students. The literary guides included in this chapter are for *Fin M'Coul, the Giant of Knockmany Hill, Jamie O'Rourke and the Big Potato,* and *Jamie O'Rourke and the Pooka.*

Enjoy the folktales and any ideas that you find helpful to you and your students.

Fin M'Coul, the Giant of Knockmany Hill

SUMMARY

Fin M'Coul and his lovely wife Oonagh are giants who lived on the top of Knockmany Hill in Ireland. One day, while building a causeway to Scotland, Fin hears that the strongest giant known in their part of the world, Cucullin, is coming to beat him up. He gets ready to run from Cucullin once again, until Oonagh says, "enough is enough." With the help of her magic fairies and a lot of cleverness, Oonagh helps Fin outwit Cucullin and prevent him from beating up anyone ever again.

PRE-READING ACTIVITIES

Create a Semantic Map

This story, as the title says, is about Fin M'Coul, the giant of Knockmany Hill. To help children enjoy and understand a new story, it is always a good idea to start with something they already know. Most students will be familiar with "Jack and the Beanstalk" stories and will have some ideas about what giants are like.

Semantic maps are used to build students' vocabulary and to activate and organize their background knowledge of a given topic. To make a semantic map, write a word that is central to the story on the board or on a piece of chart paper. In this instance, write the word "giants" and circle it. See below:

GIANTS

Next, suggest other categories that are central to the topic of giants being discussed. Add the categories of stories, sayings, and descriptions (you and your students may have others) to the map by outlining the new categories and drawing lines from them to the word "giant" in the center. See below:

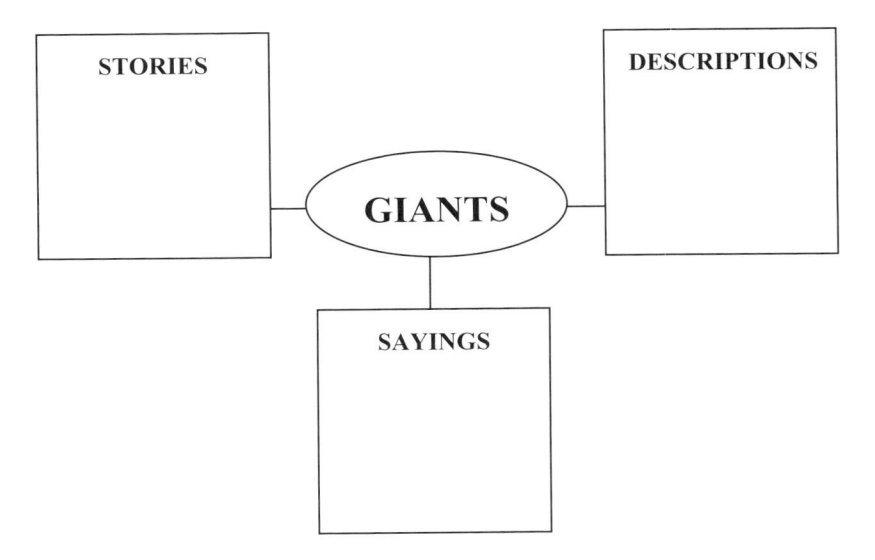

STORIES

DESCRIPTIONS

GIANTS

SAYINGS

Ask children what words, phrases, or ideas come to mind that might fit into each category. List them inside the category shapes. As children provide phrases and ideas, ask them where they learned the information or why they made their assumptions about giants. As you fill in the semantic map, it may begin to look something like this:

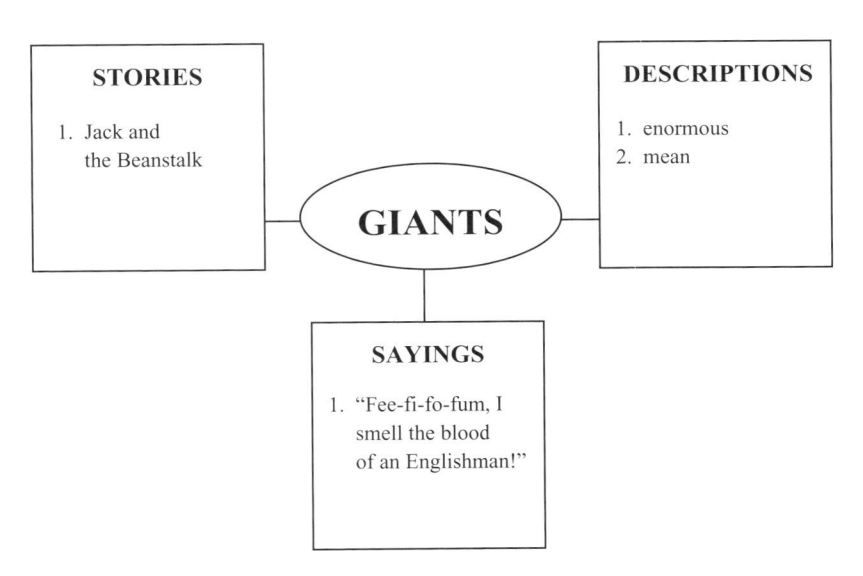

STORIES
1. Jack and the Beanstalk

DESCRIPTIONS
1. enormous
2. mean

GIANTS

SAYINGS
1. "Fee-fi-fo-fum, I smell the blood of an Englishman!"

Return to this semantic map later after reading *Fin M'Coul, the Giant of Knockmany Hill*, as children may be surprised by the kind of giant Fin is. And because of their experience with this story, their future semantic maps regarding giants will include different information.

Note: For more information about semantic maps, consult the book *Literature-based Reading Activities*, by Ruth Helena and Hallie Kay Yopp.

MAKING PREDICTIONS

Show the front and back cover of *Fin M'Coul, the Giant of Knockmany Hill* to your class and have the students make predictions about the story:

- Who do you think Fin M'Coul is and what do you think his name means?
- Where do you think Knockmany Hill is located? Do you think it could be a real place?
- What do you think the story will be about? Do you think it could be another version of "Jack and the Beanstalk?" Why or why not?
- Do giants really exist?

READING THE STORY

Read and enjoy the story of *Fin M'Coul, the Giant of Knockmany Hill* with your class. Give children ample time to look at the pictures because there are so many little details in Tomie dePaola's illustrations. If they observe carefully, children will notice the little fairies and magic folk amid the huge giants and their belongings.

- How accurate were your predictions? Did the story and characters turn out as expected?
- How would you describe Fin, Oonagh, and Cucullin? Do they fit easily into our semantic map about giants? What information do we need to add to our semantic map now that we know about three more giants?
- Why is Fin so afraid of Cucullin? What kind of reputation does Cucullin have?
- Why do you think Oonagh says, "Fin, husband of mine, enough is enough?"
- How does Oonagh help Fin beat Cucullin?
- In what ways is Oonagh even stronger than Fin or Cucullin?
- What other characters do you notice in Tomie dePaola's illustrations? How are they important to the story?

SHARING PERSONAL EXPERIENCES

- Have you ever been afraid that someone was going to beat you up? Who was it and what did you do? Did that person have a reputation like Cucullin of being a bully?
- Perhaps you were (are) the bully! How did you become one and who were you ready to beat up? How did these people react to you?

RESPONDING TO THE TEXT: WRITING

Other Endings for *Fin M'Coul* Tales

Children can write or draw other ways Fin and Oonagh could have outwitted Cucullin. What else might Oonagh have done? Or what may have happened if Fin hadn't made it back to Knockmany Hill before Cucullin arrived?

Writing a Giant Postcard

Children can write a giant postcard using tagboard to congratulate Fin and Oonagh on beating Cucullin. You may want to show your class some of the postcard examples in *The Jolly Postman or Other People's Letters,* by Janet and Allan Ahlberg, prior to having children write their own.

Writing Folktales

There are many folktales written about Fin M'Coul that have been handed down from generation to generation. Find other Fin M'Coul stories to share with your children and then have them write their own folktales about him. Children can create a new Fin M'Coul folktale as a whole class, with you as the recorder, or they can work in small groups to create ideas about Fin on their own.

To assist children in creating their own folktale, help them by pointing out some common folktale elements (see sample chart as a way of sharing the elements more easily with your class).

Children can make up folktales of their own. Help older children by sharing this chart with some of the most common elements found in folktales.

If children have heard a variety of folktales, they may want to write some of their own. Older children can use the checklist at the end of this literary guide to rate the folktales they read and to assist them in writing their own. (See p. 87.)

The following information is adapted from *A Critical Handbook of Children's Literature,* by Rebecca J. Lukens.

Irish Words and Phrases

Children list and research the original meanings or locations of some of the Irish words and places used in *Fin M'Coul, the Giant of Knockmany Hill*. Examples of some words to look up, define, write, and/or draw include: glens, leprechauns, fairies, broth, Knockmany Hill, lass, causeway, and soda bread.

Point of View

Children can see fairies and "wee folk" roaming around in the pictures that Tomie dePaola has created. Have children write about the experience of watching the giants Fin, Oonagh, and Cucullin from another point of view, such as the wee folk. Remind them to include things they might hear, smell, and feel as well as what they see.

Children can also write about events in their own lives from this point of view.

Common Elements of Folktales

Characters: Usually good and bad characters that are easily recognized—Fin and Cucullin.

Plot: Conflict centers around person versus person, person versus animal, or person versus nature. Example:—Jack versus the giant in "Jack and the Beanstalk," Fin versus Cucullin in *Fin M'Coul, the Giant of Knockmany Hill*. The climax comes near the end of the story and the ending is brief such as, "They lived happily ever after." In *Fin M'Coul, the Giant of Knockmany Hill,* the story ends with "And they lived a long happy life." Action is fast and lively—the heart of the folktale.

Theme: Usually concerns characters' human needs or wishes. For example, in "Jack and the Beanstalk," Jack wants to steal the hen so he and his mother won't have to worry about money. In *Fin M'Coul,* Fin wants to escape being beaten up by Cucullin and Oonagh wants to stop moving around because Fin is afraid of being beaten up.

Evil: Often good versus evil; good is rewarded and evil is punished. Fin (the good giant) wins; Cucullin (the bad giant) loses.

RESPONDING TO THE TEXT: ART AND WRITING

Thinking Bubbles

This strategy, from Brownlie, Close, and Wingren, "invites students into the minds of story characters and has them represent their thinking in cartoon illustrations using the inside and outside voices of the characters. The teacher reads the text to the students and stops three or four times to have them 'show me what's happening.'"

I have used this strategy when first introducing a book to children. I find that it is very useful for reinforcing students' comprehension and understanding of what happens in stories that have been read to them a second or third time.

Steps in using the "Thinking Bubbles" strategy

1. Invite children to share with you how a cartoonist indicates that someone is speaking in a cartoon strip. Draw a "speaking bubble" on the board.

2. Now have children share how a cartoonist indicates what characters are thinking in a comic strip, or using an inside voice. Draw a "thinking bubble" on the board:

3. Discuss how sometimes characters say one thing but may be thinking something else.

4. Give each child a piece of 8½" × 11" paper and have them divide it into four equal boxes. Tell them that you will reread *Fin M'Coul, the Giant of Knockmany Hill* and stop at four different places in the story. When you stop, ask them to draw the characters in the story and include what the characters may be saying (speaking bubbles) and thinking (thinking bubbles). If time permits, they can include other details they remember up to that point. Children can use regular pencils to sketch and fill in with color later, if desired.

Note: Encourage children by stressing that their drawings do not have to be their best; they should focus on the characters and what they are saying and thinking. Often, if children draw the characters in this way, when they return later to the drawings, they easily remember details that they can add to the scene or setting of the story.

Possible places to stop in your reading and have children draw

1. Read to the point where it says, "But this time, Cucullin was sure to get him. So Fin left the causeway and sped off for Knockmany Hill, his house, and his darling Oonagh."

2. Continue to the part where "Knockmany Hill gave a little dance. 'He's coming!' said Fin, his face turning a fine shade of pale green." (Encourage children to draw both Fin and Oonagh.)

3. Continue to the point where Cucullin says, "'THIS WAS a thunderbolt, until I caught it and flattened it. And that's what I'm goin' to do to Fin M'Coul too.'" "'Tsk-tsk,' said Oonagh. 'That may not be as easy as you think. Fin M'Coul is a big broth of a man. Why take a look at our little baby and you might be gettin' an idea of the strength and breadth of Fin himself.'" (Encourage children to include Oonagh, Cucullin, and Fin.)

4. Finally, stop at the point near the ending where it says, "With a strong bite, Fin M'Coul bit the brass finger right off. Then up Fin leapt and began to pound the daylights out of poor, weak Cucullin. That was that."

You may want to stop at many more points—just have children use both sides of the paper. There are so many great places in the story to stop—especially to record Cucullin's reactions to the baby, the squeezing of the rock (egg), and the many times his teeth are broken off from biting into the "frying pan bread"! Children enjoy drawing these sketches and the characters' words and thoughts. And this activity effectively demonstrates their comprehension of what is happening throughout the story. Children have fun sharing their cartoons with others in the class. They often begin to use thinking and speaking bubbles in other work they do.

RESPONDING TO THE TEXT: DRAMA

Readers Theatre

Children can have great fun acting out the story. They can divide up parts of the story and read directly from multiple copies of the book while others act out the parts of Fin, Oonagh, and Cucullin. If you give children a little extra time, I'm sure they will come up with some great props for Fin to use when dressed up like Baby Fin. How will they convince others that they are supposed to be giants?

Puppet Show

Children can also make puppet characters using materials like paper bags, socks, felt, sticks, paper plates, and papier-mâché. They can then rehearse and share the puppet show with the rest of the class.

Children may also want to write their own puppet show script and include a part for a narrator. Or, divide up parts of the story and have small groups act out each part.

RESPONDING TO THE TEXT: ART

Think Big!

Children can paint "giant" murals! They can divide the story into parts and paint and design giant murals that can be displayed throughout the classroom or school. It will be especially fun for them if the mural is taller than they are! This will help them identify with the concept of "giant." Children may actually want to invite tall adults into the classroom and trace them, to be sure they are creating a "giant" mural.

Extensions

Children can choose a few scenes from the story and create their own Giant Big Book about Fin M'Coul. You can use tagboard for the pages and a variety of art media, such as collage, tempera paint, or other art techniques.

Or the class can divide up scenes from *Fin M'Coul, the Giant of Knockmany Hill* and small groups can develop illustrations to depict each scene.

Painting Kid Giants

Children can outline themselves and paint their "characters" as they might look if they were in the story of *Fin M'Coul, the Giant of Knockmany Hill*. Encourage them to assume the posture of someone in the story and appear to be moving or eating or walking. Or a group of children can get together and use their giant characters to create one of the scenes from the book.

Sell or Design a New House for Fin and Oonagh

Now that Fin doesn't have to worry about watching out for Cucullin anymore, he doesn't have to live on the top of Knockmany Hill, "the windiest of hills." Children can pretend that they are realtors and get ready to sell the ideal house to Fin and Oonagh. Or, as contractors, they can try to convince them to build their dream home!

As realtors...

Children will need to come up with a flyer advertising the home, where it is located, complete with pictures, descriptions of floor plans, the plot of land it is on, schools nearby, and features that would attract the giants to purchase the home they are trying to sell.

As contractors...

Children will need to think about the qualities Oonagh and Fin might look for in an ideal house and try to design one. Of course, a sketch of the home and a floor plan will need to be included.

Children contractors can "build" the house model using cardboard boxes and paint or other construction materials. Since attention to detail will be necessary, children may want to collaborate in groups, much like a contracting firm.

Children may want to use dollhouse furniture and accessories in creating their house models.

Frying Pans

Bring in cast-iron frying pans from home (or request some from parents of your students) and let children lift and experience how heavy they are. These are the pans that are hidden inside the bread that Cucullin bites into. Challenge children to try and design bread-shaped box or papier-mâché sculptures around the frying pans like Oonagh made. Or, they may come up with their own "Irish" ideas for tricking Cucullin.

Irish Art

Older children can learn a lot about Celtic artwork by studying the jewelry and metalwork designs used by Tomie dePaola in the borders of the book. Much Celtic artwork is influenced by the Catholic Church; the most magnificent achievement in Irish Celtic art is the *Book of Kells*. Find examples of

Folktale Checklist

NAME _____ DATE _____

Title of Folktake	✓ here	Examples from the folktale
Does the folktale have these elements? ✓check those that apply		
Characters good or bad?		
Plot Conflict person vs. person? Or person vs. animal? or person vs. nature?		
Climax brief and at the end?		
Action fast and lively?		
Theme about needs or wishes? and/or good vs. evil?		
Rating How did the folktale rate? (give one point for every check)		

artwork from the *Book of Kells* and other Irish Celtic art and encourage children to look for similar motifs in *Fin M'Coul, the Giant of Knockmany Hill.* Have them experiment using some of the many scrolls or repeating patterns that appear in the book.

As a variation, bring in samples of illuminated letters and have children try to create their first initials using the samples as a guide. Or, teach them how to write their first initial using calligraphy. For more information about the *Book of Kells,* your children may enjoy reading, *The Sailor Who Captured the Sea: A Story of the Book of Kells,* by Deborah Nourse Lattimore.

RESPONDING TO THE TEXT: IRISH MUSIC

There is an abundance of wonderful Celtic music available to share with your children. Teachers and children can bring in audiotapes or CDs of favorite Irish music to share and to learn familiar Irish songs.

Note: I like to play Irish background music while children are working on these projects. They really enjoy it and often begin to hum along!

Jamie O'Rourke and the Big Potato

SUMMARY

"Jamie O'Rourke is the laziest man in all of Ireland!" He will do anything to avoid working, especially in his potato garden. One day he captures a leprechaun, who grants him a single wish. What does Jamie wish for but the biggest pratie (potato) in all the world. No more potato planting for Jamie! The results of planting the gigantic pratie are hysterical and it takes Jamie's wife, Eileen, to come up with a solution that saves the day (and Jamie's lazy way of life!).

Tomie dePaola read a short Irish tale that gave him the inspiration for *Jamie O'Rourke and the Big Potato*. He was reminded of the many times his grandfather, Thomas Lawrence Downey, would share stories and Irish tales with him when he was young. When reading the original tale, he could almost hear his grandfather whispering in his ear, "Jamie O'Rourke is the laziest man . . ."

PRE-READING ACTIVITIES

Creating a K-W-L

To activate prior knowledge and to find out what children know about leprechauns and Ireland, brainstorm and list all of those things children know or think they know on a K-W-L (**K**now-**W**ant to learn-**L**earned) chart. (See example.) List their ideas on chart paper or newsprint and display the chart somewhere where children can add to it in the future. Return to this chart for additions and changes as your Irish unit continues and children gain insight and knowledge.

MAKING PREDICTIONS

Show the front and back cover of *Jamie O'Rourke and the Big Potato* to the children and have them make predictions about the story:

What we know:	What we want to learn:	What we have learned:

- Which character do you think is Jamie O'Rourke? the leprechaun? What information do you already know that helped you to make your predictions?
- Why do you think the book is called *Jamie O'Rourke and the Big Potato*? What do potatoes have to do with Ireland?
- Have you ever heard of potatoes growing larger than a human being?
- The potato grew to be so large! What might have happened?
- Do you think this is a true story? Why or why not?

Note: You may want to spend a little time during the activities discussing how potatoes came to Ireland and why Irish people are thought to eat them a lot. See some Background on Potatoes section at the end of this literary guide.

READING THE STORY

Read and enjoy *Jamie O'Rourke and the Big Potato* with your class.

THINKING CRITICALLY ABOUT THE TEXT

- Why do you think Jamie O'Rourke is so lazy?
- How would you describe his wife Eileen?
- Describe the leprechaun Jamie caught. How is he clever in dealing with Jamie?
- What problems does Jamie face in growing such a huge pratie?
- Could a potato grow that large in real life? How much do you think the largest potato ever grown might have weighed?
- The villagers are happy to take pieces of the huge potato home with them. Why are they so eager to help out?
- Do you think Jamie or Eileen know that people will tire of eating potatoes all of the time and won't want Jamie to plant the potato eye he has saved? Why or why not?

SHARING PERSONAL EXPERIENCES

When did you first learn about leprechauns or hear about Ireland? Did you hear about them from a grandparent, like Tomie dePaola did, or from someone or somewhere else? Ask children to discuss the books or people who have taught them about Ireland or leprechauns. If they are of Irish descent, some may have grown up believing in leprechauns. Others may have learned about them through oral storytelling or through books or movies. Give children time to share their stories with one another.

90 ♥ On the Wing of a Whitebird

RESPONDING TO THE TEXT: WRITING

Letters to Eileen

When Eileen wrenches her back planting potatoes, the village women say that "St. Bridget and the Virgin Mary herself must have smiled on Eileen O'Rourke. . . . Why it's the first rest she's had since she married Jamie O'Rourke." Have children pretend they are one of the villagers and write a get well card for Eileen.

Making Lists

Eileen can't do a lot of the housework when she is confined to bed. Make a list of things for Jamie to do while Eileen is recuperating. Children can also make a list of things Eileen could do to keep from getting bored while staying in bed all day.

Persuasive Letter Writing

Children write a letter to Jamie convincing him that it's time for him to help out a lot more around the house now that Eileen is hurt.

Making Wishes

Children write a different ending for the story based on Jamie wishing for something else rather than the "biggest pratie in all the world." How does the story change?

Another Point of View

Children write the story based on Eileen's discovering the leprechaun and making a wish. What would she have wished for and how would that have changed the story?

Leprechaun Stories

Children go back to their brainstorming list (the K-W-L) of what they know and think about leprechauns. They write their own stories about what they would wish for if they caught a leprechaun. Would they want his pot of gold or want their wish(es) to be granted? What would they do with the granted wish and/or the leprechaun?

A great follow up to *Jamie O'Rourke and the Big Potato* is *Strega Nona,* by Tomie dePaola. What happens to Big Anthony when he gets his wish and the pasta pot produces enough pasta for all the townspeople and more?

Irish Dialect and Word Fun

Tomie dePaola drops some of the "g's" in his writing and uses some Irish phrases to suggest Irish dialect in the story of *Jamie O'Rourke and the Big Potato*. Have children read through the book again and list some of the words and phrases the author uses and then list any other Irish phrases they may have heard. They can also experiment with other words of their own, having fun dropping the "g" at the end of words and sharing their words with others in class. Examples from *Jamie O'Rourke and the Big Potato*:

Words:	Phrases:
knowin'	"Sure and I wouldn't be <u>knowin</u>'"
tellin'	"There's no <u>tellin</u>' how soon old
knockin'	Death will be <u>knockin</u>' on me door."
	"Oh, the saints preserve us"

Creating Songs

Children create a song about the story to sing to a familiar tune such as "Row, Row, Row Your Boat," "Old McDonald Had a Farm," or "Three Blind Mice." They can work in groups to create them, write them, and rehearse and then present them to the rest of the class. This activity is lots of fun, and when the songs are shared, children find them hysterically funny.

The following are some examples of songs my students experimented with when reading *Jamie O'Rourke and the Big Potato*. These could be put into some kind of a graphic for sharing.

To the tune of "Three Blind Mice"

Jamie O'Rourke, Jamie O'Rourke,
Caught a leprechaun, caught a leprechaun.
He gave up gold for a pratie seed.
He watered and hoed and picked some weeds.
And then he got lots of feed.
That Jamie O'Rourke!

To the tune of "Mary Had a Little Lamb"

Jamie caught a leprechaun, leprechaun, leprechaun,
Jamie caught a leprechaun and got a pratie seed.

Extensions

After children write their songs they can design costumes:

- to go with the characters in their songs and act out the song as they sing, or
- "become" an Irish singing group and share the songs they have written

RESPONDING TO THE TEXT: INTEGRATED LANGUAGE ARTS

Solving the Potato Problem

Children write and draw different ways that Jamie and the villagers could have moved the giant pratie. They try to think of other tools they could use, animals that might help out, and so forth.

Potato Recipes

The villagers get very tired of eating potatoes with every meal. Give children, in cooperative groups, a blank calendar form. Have them list a different potato dish for each day of the month. Give them time to research potato recipes from cookbooks you have brought in or that they bring in from home or the library.

Class Recipe Book

These recipes can be copied by children (each child chooses a different recipe), illustrated with Celtic borders, and bound into a classroom collection of potato recipes to share with the students' families.

Cookbook Covers

Children use potatoes to make a potato print cover for their cookbook. (See ideas that follow in the Art response section).

Cookbook Sections

For one section of the recipe book, children brainstorm a list of what they would put on the top of baked potatoes. Encourage them to be creative. Have them make a bar graph to determine the most popular toppings. If health codes permit, have your own baked potato bar at school for lunch some day!

Potatoes and People!

How are potatoes and people alike? For one thing, both have "eyes" and skin. Since the toy Mr. Potato Head is still available, thanks to the recent *Toy Story* movies, ask someone to bring it in. Did you know that, originally, no potato body was sold with the Mr. Potato Head sets? Children supplied a real potato for the bodies. But when mothers continued to find stale, moldy, old potatoes rotting under furniture and behind radiators, they complained loudly enough for the company to include the body in the next generation of Mr. Potato Heads. For more information on the fascinating history of Mr. Potato Head, consult *The Amazing Potato Book,* by Paulette Bourgeois.

Character Display

Children choose Jamie, Eileen, or the leprechaun to create a character display. These character displays are a visual representation of the character surrounded by descriptive words and phrases that describe him or her. The descriptions are then supported by written lines or phrases from the actual text itself. Do this as a whole class with younger children or model the steps for older children. See diagram and steps listed below:

1. Give children a large piece of paper—at least 9" × 12"—to create the character chosen. Encourage children to draw their character, cut it out, and decorate it with crayons, markers, or paint.

2. Next, have them glue the finished character to the center of a large piece of butcher paper—about 3'× 3'.

3. Have children write at least five adjectives or descriptive phrases that pertain to their character on index cards.

4. Below the cards, have children find sentences and phrases from *Jamie O'Rourke and the Big Potato* that support their descriptive words and phrases. Have them write these on lined paper (for ease in writing) or on "speaking bubbles" cut out from large white paper if the descriptive phrases are quotes. Glue them near the index card words or near the character if speaking bubbles are created.

5. Display the characters where all can see them in the classroom.

Note: These descriptive character displays can also be created by small groups of children to speed up the creation process. (See p. 94.)

RESPONDING TO THE TEXT: SCIENCE

Potatoes, Potatoes!

Ask students what they know about potatoes and record or sketch these facts and ideas. You might ask them:

- Where are potatoes grown?
- How many different kinds of potatoes are there?
- How do potatoes grow? How are they planted? How often are they harvested?
- Why are potatoes associated with Ireland?
- Where were the first potatoes found?

Have children research some of their questions and draw a poster showing answers they find. Children can share pictures that might explain their new knowledge to their classmates. The poster can be taped together using book tape to form an accordion-style big book or they can be displayed at eye level throughout the classroom for other children to read. The answers to some of these questions can be found in *The Amazing Potato: A Story in Which the Incas, Conquistadors, Marie Antoinette, Thomas Jefferson, Wars, Famines, Immigrants, and French Fries All Play a Part,* by Milton Meltzer. This book is appropriate for intermediate children. Excerpts could be used with younger children.

Sorting Potatoes

Children visit their local grocery stores or farmer's market and bring in various kinds of potatoes for sorting. They can sort potatoes by best kinds for baking, for boiling, and so on. They can also sort potatoes by color, size, and shape. Consult the two potato books previously suggested for helpful information. Children can also create a map that shows where the most popular types of potatoes are grown.

Nutrition

Potatoes are often called a wonder food. Have a committee of children research the nutritional benefits of potatoes to share with the rest of the class.

Planting Potatoes

After students learn and teach each other about how potatoes grow, you might want to take the opportunity (climate and time permitting) to plant some potatoes. If you have access to garden space

A Whiner

"Oh, poor me," wailed Jamie. "I'll starve to death. I'd best go to church and confess to Father O'Malley."

Selfish

"Why, what should I wish for? Me who's about to die of starvation because…"

Lazy

"He would do anything to avoid working, especially if it had to do with growing potatoes."

Clever

"I saved a potato eye for a seed and it's just about time to plant it."

around your school, you can plant potatoes and chart their growth. You might want to invite a gardener or farmer to share planting tips with your children.

Children can also plant their own potatoes indoors by using toothpicks to suspend a sweet potato over a jar of water. Set the sweet potato on a sunny windowsill and have children observe and chart its growth.

RESPONDING TO THE TEXT: ART

Creating Leprechauns

Using paint, lots of green paper, and any other art materials on hand, have children create their own life-sized leprechaun. Remind them that they are known as "wee folk," or "little people," so they won't be very large. You might have them return to the class K-W-L before they begin so that they have some specific details to include.

Creating Leprechaun Traps

One year on St. Patrick's Day, I had a friend paint tiny green footprints (using a footprint stamp she had made) all over our classroom. She also turned over some furniture and did silly little mischievous things that leprechauns are known to do. My third and fourth graders were delighted, and because I hadn't done it and wasn't there when it was done, I could claim innocence!

My children decided that they wanted time to create leprechaun traps in case the leprechauns returned. It was hysterical to observe the creation processes that ensued with boxes and recycled materials. Your children are sure to have fun with this idea. Remember, catching a leprechaun is not easy!

Potato Prints

Many teachers like to use potatoes as a printing tool because they are both easy to use and affordable. Children can use plastic knives to carve a pattern out of half a potato. Tempera paint prints easily on construction paper. Children can print borders, patterns, and designs to make book covers, the recipe book covers mentioned earlier, or murals and other displays.

For an outstanding example of what can be done with potato prints, share the counting book *One Potato: A Counting Book of Potato Prints,* by Diana Pomeroy.

A Jamie O'Rourke Mural

Have children work in small groups to design one large mural for the story or several small murals showing different scenes. Using various potato prints, have children see if they can create a variety of textures on their mural(s). These murals are a good tool to use when you want children to capture a particular scene in a story. They can revisit the story to get ideas on adding details.

Jamie O'Rourke and the Pooka

Note: Jamie O'Rourke and the Pooka is the sequel to *Jamie O'Rourke and the Big Potato.* I suggest you share the books in order with your children if possible, as you learn a lot about the character of Jamie O'Rourke in the first book.

Some Background on Potatoes

During the 1530s Spanish conquerors set out to raid the Inca villages of Peru in search of gold, silver, and other precious metals. In one of the villages the Spanish didn't find any precious metals, but they found an abundance of maize (corn), beans, and an unusual vegetable—the potato—they had never seen before. Although initially they weren't impressed with this funny looking vegetable, the conquerors gradually discovered its importance in the daily diets of the Incas.

The Spanish did find many precious metals in other raids, and it was their custom to melt down the metals and ship them back to Spain. It is thought that the Spanish packed potatoes on board their ships to feed the sailors on the long voyages home, and that is how the potato arrived in Europe.

In 1588 a great Spanish fleet set out to conquer England. Unexpectedly, they were defeated by the English Navy and proceeded to retreat. A great storm rose off the coast of Ireland and many ships sank or were captured. In boarding the captured ships, the Irish discovered that potatoes were among the "treasures" and they probably planted them in coastal communities. That is how many people believe the potato first came to the Emerald Isle.

The Irish learned that the potato was not only nutritious but also easy to plant and harvest. It quickly became a staple of the people, who at that time were starving and involved in many wars. The potato saved many from starvation, although the great famine of Ireland was yet to come.

For more information on the history and importance of the potato, read *The Amazing Potato: A Story in Which the Incas, Conquistadors, Marie Antoinette, Thomas Jefferson, Wars, Famines, Immigrants, and French Fries All Play a Part,* by Milton Meltzer.

SUMMARY

Jamie O'Rourke is still the laziest man in all of Ireland! He will do anything to avoid work and loves to pass the time taking long naps in the front of his home. His wife, Eileen, who does all of the cooking and cleaning, wakes him up from a nap to explain what he needs to do in the house while she goes to be with her sister who has just had a baby. Immediately after Eileen leaves, Jamie gets into bed to sleep. A knock on the door interrupts Jamie's plan and brings in his cronies, who have come to eat, drink, and laugh the night away. They leave a huge mess for Jamie to clean up in the morning. Imagine Jamie's surprise when a pooka shows up in the middle of the night to do the cleaning—oh my! Will Jamie ever learn to clean up after himself?

PRE-READING ACTIVITIES
MAKING PREDICTIONS

If you previously read *Jamie O'Rourke and the Big Potato*:

- What do we already know about Jamie O'Rourke? What do you remember from our reading of *Jamie O'Rourke and the Big Potato*?

If you are reading this Jamie O'Rourke book first:

- Who do you think Jamie O'Rourke is? How would you describe him?

Other prediction questions:

- Looking at the front cover, what emotions do you see on Jamie O'Rourke's face?
- Why do you think he feels those feelings?
- What do you think this story is going to be about?

What is a Pooka?

Encourage your children to brainstorm and list their ideas about what a pooka might be. List their ideas on a chart and refer back to it after reading the story.

What Does a Pooka Look Like?

Share the front and the back book covers with children. Also, read the author's note at the end of the book to give some hints as to what a pooka might be and why it might come to visit Jamie O'Rourke. Have children sketch what they think Tomie dePaola's version of a *pooka* might look like.

Thinking Critically about the Text

- Why do you think Jamie goes to bed right after Eileen leaves?
- What changes his plans?
- Do you think that Jamie's friends are as lazy as Jamie? Why or why not? What clues can you find from the story to support your answer?
- How would you describe a pooka? Do you think all pookas look alike?
- Why does the pooka show up at Jamie's house night after night?

- Why and how do you think Jamie musters up the courage to talk with the pooka? Is it like Jamie to think about others?
- Does Jamie expect the pooka to leave before cleaning up his mess?

RESPONDING TO THE TEXT: CLASS MEETING DISCUSSION

Kindnesses

Jamie is very thoughtful in sharing his coat with the pooka. What are some ways others have been kind to you lately or you have been kind to a friend? Share some of these in a class meeting with each other.

RESPONDING TO THE TEXT: WRITING

A Letter to Eileen

Write a letter from Jamie to Eileen, before she returns home, in which he tries to explain about the pooka. What would Jamie say in the letter? Do you think Eileen would believe his story?

A Letter Back to Jamie

Imagine Eileen getting a letter from Jamie explaining that the house is a mess because a pooka didn't clean it up! How do you think she'd respond?

Eileen's Way . . .

Write another ending for the story but have Eileen win this time. How does she win? What should Eileen do with Jamie at the end of the story?

A Lazy List

List all of the jobs you tend to be lazy about. Okay—be honest! How about washing the dishes, walking the dog, doing your homework? See if you can come up with five to ten activities you would rather not do and share that list with a friend. Are any activities on both of your lists?

My Very Own Pooka

Why would a pooka stop by to help you? Might it need to help you clean up your room? do the dishes or empty the dishwasher? take out the garbage that is piling up? How long might it take the pooka to finish all of your work? Write about why a pooka would visit you and what you hope would happen while it was there.

Gifts for a Pooka

If you wrote about a pooka above, think what kind of gift it might appreciate. What could you give that would make it happy?

RESPONDING TO THE TEXT: ART

Design Your Own Pooka

Children can create their own pooka. Give them large, 12" × 18" paper to sketch their pooka first, and then let them choose an art medium to make the pooka come alive! They might choose to decorate their pooka using paint, watercolor crayons, crayons, or colored pencils, to name a few ideas. Children may also choose to bring in a fabric scrap to make a coat or other clothing item for their pooka.

Add to the Mural

Add to the mural created for *Jamie O'Rourke and the Big Potato* or begin a new one for this story. See directions listed previously in this chapter.

Pookas on Display

You might create a mural or bulletin board to display all of the pookas created by your students. They could have a "Pooka Party" or be "Pookas on Parade!"

Chapter 4

The *Bill and Pete* Stories

INTRODUCTION

The *Bill and Pete* stories are delightful, funny stories about two friends, a crocodile named William Everett and his Egyptian plover toothpick named Pete. They are great to use during the first weeks of school as a way to encourage children to form new friendships and to honor old ones already formed. No matter when you share the *Bill and Pete* stories with your class, children will delight in their adventures. Titles in the series include *Bill and Pete, Bill and Pete Go Down the Nile,* and *Bill and Pete to the Rescue.*

Bill and Pete

SUMMARY

Bill and Pete is the story of two good friends, a crocodile named William Everett and his bird toothbrush named Pete. Children and adults alike delight in this story inspired by the Egyptian plover that actually picks out food from crocodile teeth! As William Everett begins his first day of crocodile school, Pete is always by his side. The story takes place along the Nile River and makes us laugh aloud as Bill and Pete become fast friends and also end up saving the day.

PRE-READING ACTIVITIES

Creating a K-W-L

To activate prior knowledge and to find out what children already know about crocodiles and the area around the Nile River, brainstorm and list all of those things children know or think that they know on a K-W-L (**K**now-**W**ant to learn-**L**earned) chart. (See example on p. 89.) List ideas on chart paper or newsprint and display the chart somewhere where children can add to it in the future as all *Bill and Pete* stories are shared.

Ask children what questions they have regarding crocodiles and the Nile River.

- "What would you like to learn more about?"

Write those questions down in the column, "What we *want* to learn." Return to this chart later after reading the story and after children have done their own research. Leave room for children to add new facts and any additional questions that surface.

MAKING PREDICTIONS

Show the front and the back cover of *Bill and Pete* to the children and have them make predictions about the story:

- Which character do you think is Bill? Pete? Why? Does it matter?
- Are the names of characters important in stories?
- Can you find clues on the front and back cover that tell about when and where the story takes place?

READING THE STORY

Read *Bill and Pete* with your class. Children find parts of the story hysterically funny, especially the ending!

THINKING CRITICALLY ABOUT THE TEXT

- What new skills does William Everett learn at school?
- There is a saying that "practice make perfect." Do you think that William Everett would agree with the saying after trying to write his name so many times?
- What is a nickname? Are other children in William Everett's class trying to write their full names or their nicknames? Use the book to check your answer.
- What are some ways Pete is a good friend to William Everett?
- Could this story happen in real life? Why or why not? Find details in the book to support your answer.

SHARING PERSONAL EXPERIENCES

Children like to discuss this book because Tomie dePaola has provided such humorous illustrations and text. Give children time to discuss the friendship formed by these unlikely animal friends and then have them share some of their own special friendship stories.

RESPONDING TO THE TEXT: INTEGRATED LANGUAGE ARTS—REFERENCE SKILLS

Note the words "ibis" and "Cairo." Find sentences in *Bill and Pete* that use these words. Read them aloud and then put them on the chalkboard or on some type of overhead projector.

Examples: "The little crocodiles repeated after *Ms. Ibis*."
"That's the Bad Guy, and those crocodiles are on their way to *Cairo*—to become suitcases," said an old crocodile swimming by."

Have dictionaries or encyclopedias (either books or electronic) at your side to model looking up the word "ibis." If you look the word up in a primary dictionary or encyclopedia, it may not be listed because an ibis is an unusual bird. You may need to borrow a dictionary or encyclopedia from a classroom of older grade or use an electronic encyclopedia for older students. This is good modeling for children because in editing their own writing and doing their own research, they need to know that answers are not always in one book. Sometimes, it is necessary to search through other books or reference materials for answers.

Talk your way through the research process, stating why you need to know how to use the alphabet to find the letter "i" in the dictionary and encyclopedia and discuss the layout of the reference books.

When you succeed in finding the definition of the word "ibis," read it aloud. Explain that not all character names are going to be found in the dictionary, but Ms. Ibis's name can be because Tomie dePaola cleverly named William Everett's teacher after an actual bird found in the Nile River area.

Do the same thing by looking up the word "Cairo" in the dictionary or encyclopedia. Read its definition and have students use a map or globe to find and point out where Cairo, Egypt, and the Nile River are.

It is helpful to model using the dictionary and other reference materials in front of children. Even younger or nonreading children will learn from our example about the printed materials at their disposal and will more likely access them in the future.

RESPONDING TO THE TEXT: WRITING

Make a Friendship Web

Together with the class, make a web with the words "good friend" in the center (see example below). Brainstorm qualities of a good friend and write these words around the center circle. Children can use the adjectives from the web to do some of the following activities.

Write stories

Write about a good friend. Write a story about special times spent together with that friend or simply describe that person.

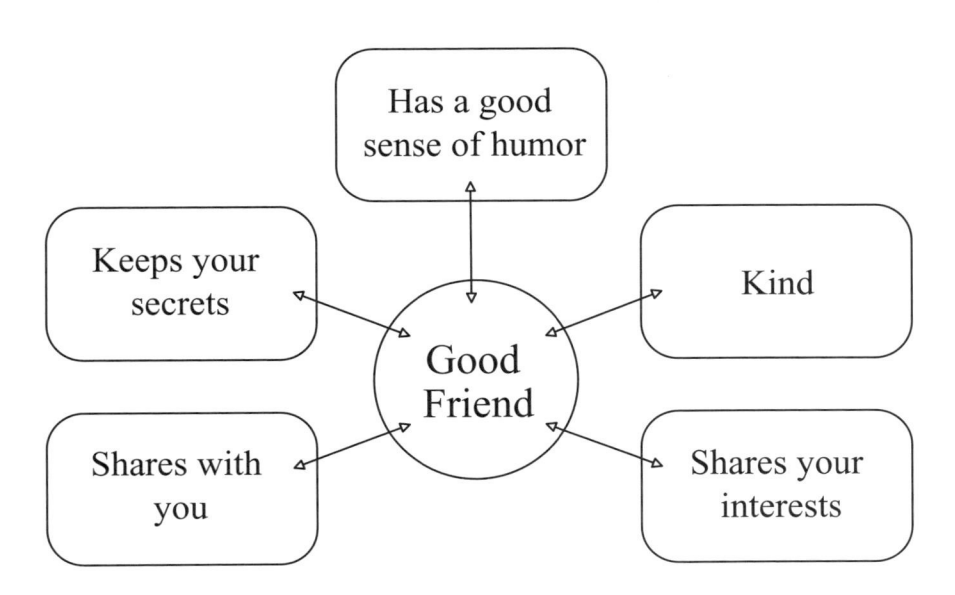

```
                    ┌──────────────┐
                    │  Has a good  │
                    │sense of humor│
                    └──────┬───────┘
                           ↓
┌───────────┐          ╱───────╲          ┌──────┐
│Keeps your │  →      │  Good   │    →    │ Kind │
│  secrets  │         │ Friend  │         └──────┘
└───────────┘          ╲───────╱
                       ↗       ↘
┌───────────┐                        ┌────────────┐
│Shares with│ →                    → │Shares your │
│    you    │                        │ interests  │
└───────────┘                        └────────────┘
```

Create riddles

Take turns making up descriptive riddles about friends in the classroom. Have children use words from the web to describe a person in the class to their classmates without giving away his or her name.

Create poems or thank-you notes

Write friendship poems or thank-you notes to special people thanking them for being such good friends.

Someday, I'd like to be known for . . .

Write something you'd like to be famous for in the future. You may want to grow up to be a famous author, basketball, or movie star. You also may want to be known for how you treat people, protect the earth, or help endangered animals.

RESPONDING TO THE TEXT: RESEARCH

Children do their own research about crocodiles or the Nile River and share that information with the rest of the class. They can make a book, display, or drawing or they can present new information orally. This activity can be done individually, committee style—researching with a few friends—or as an entire class.

RESPONDING TO THE TEXT: HANDWRITING PRACTICE

Children practice their handwriting just like Bill! Some may need to practice writing single letters while others work on writing words or creating simple poems using their very best handwriting. Because children always show growth over time, this handwriting sample can be saved in student portfolios and compared to later handwriting samples.

Bill and Pete Go Down the Nile

SUMMARY

Bill and Pete Go Down the Nile is the sequel to *Bill and Pete* that finds our two friends in school once again and preparing to go on a field trip. We learn more about the land around the Nile River: the sphinx, pyramids, mummies, sarcophaguses, and the Royal Museum. No *Bill and Pete* adventure would be complete without the Bad Guy. And when he shows up ready to steal a priceless jewel, the Sacred Eye of Isis, the fun and laughter continue!

PRE-READING ACTIVITIES

MAKING PREDICTIONS

Show children the front and back cover of the book and discuss:

- What do you think the title *Bill and Pete Go Down the Nile* means?
- Can you predict what Bill and Pete will see on their journey?

- How do the pictures on the cover help you learn about the setting? What can you tell about the land around the Nile River?

Reading the Story

Read the story *Bill and Pete Go Down the Nile* with your children. Stop during the reading to notice some of the details Tomie dePaola includes in the terrific illustrations.

THINKING CRITICALLY ABOUT THE TEXT

- What are some of the new things Bill and Pete learn at school?
- Can you tell the difference between a mummy, sarcophagus, sphinx, and a pyramid? Return to the book if you need help explaining your answer.
- What forms of transportation do Bill and Pete use on their field trip?
- What do you think the "W. C." stands for on the doors to the rest rooms? If you're not sure, how can you find out?

SHARING PERSONAL EXPERIENCES

Children share past field trip experiences they have had. They may want to write, draw, or act out their adventures.

RESPONDING TO THE TEXT: INTEGRATED LANGUAGE ARTS

Design a Field Trip for Bill and Pete

In learning more about the area around the Nile River, children write about where they think Bill and Pete will end up next. What would be another logical place for Bill and Pete to visit?

Design a Field Trip for Your Own Class

Children design their own field trip for the class. They can share where they would go on their adventure and what they would learn through writing, dictating, or drawing.

Create a Safety Manual for Bill and Pete

Children create a field trip safety manual for Bill and Pete to help prepare them for their next adventures. Have them revisit both *Bill and Pete* books to review the areas that the characters visit. Encourage children to imagine themselves as a crocodile or bird on the Nile River as they think about their safety needs.

Some steps to help prepare for a real classroom field trip

1. Read *Bill and Pete Go Down the Nile* before going on your own class trip.
2. Discuss what Bill and Pete's class do to prepare before going on their field trip to the sphinx, pyramids, and so forth.

3. List or state all of the things children have learned in preparation for going on their next field trip. Older children can record these in personal journals while you list their ideas on the board or on chart paper.

4. Together, predict all of the things your children will need to bring with them in order to go on a safe and successful field trip. Have them make a list or draw pictures with a partner of what they will need and why.

   Example:

What we need:	*Why we need it:*
lunch	we will miss lunch at school
jacket or sweater	it may be cool
a pencil and journal	to write notes and draw sketches
a backpack	to hold everything you bring

5. Invite children to share with their classmates their lists and/or pictures of what to bring on the field trip and why. Add any other items you know they may need in addition. Children can write down these items on a reminder list, or you can use children's ideas to send home a reminder note to parents prior to the field trip.

6. Before leaving on your class adventure, "walk through" the field trip verbally—from leaving the school to actually being in your destination. This gives children an idea of what to expect and how to act appropriately during their upcoming excursion. For instance, some places require quiet voices, like art museums and libraries. It helps to go over these little details in advance.

7. You may want children to take along their journals and a pencil for sketching or note taking while on the trip. They also can write or draw reflections in their journals upon their return.

Sharing our field trip experiences

When children return to school after their field trip, give them an opportunity to document what they observed and learned by having them:

- Write or dictate a story to someone about what they did or observed on their trip. This might be in the form of a letter to their parent(s) about their experience.
- Draw, sketch, or create something using any art form that shows what they learned or experienced.
- Act out a portion of the trip.
- Create a song, rap, or chant about the trip.
- Write a note to any parent volunteer who went on the field trip thanking them for his or her assistance and sharing what they learned.

RESPONDING TO THE TEXT: ART

For art ideas, see the Art response section at the end of the *Bill and Pete to the Rescue* literary guide for ideas to be used with all three *Bill and Pete* stories.

The *Bill and Pete* Stories ♥ 107

Bill and Pete to the Rescue

SUMMARY

Bill and Pete to the Rescue is the third book in the *Bill and Pete* series. Bill's cousin, little Jane Allison, is missing! It turns out that the Bad Guy's Big Bad Brother from Louisiana has taken her and other exotic animals from the Nile and is headed back on an ocean liner to America. Bill and Pete stow away on the boat, but Pete gets caught by the Rich Lady on the way! Bill hooks up with some "gators from the Louisiana bayou" when they arrive, determined to rescue both Pete and little Jane Allison.

PRE-READING ACTIVITIES

MAKING PREDICTIONS

Show the front and the back cover of *Bill and Pete to the Rescue* to your class and have them make predictions about the story. The Bad Guy was caught and put in jail in the previous *Bill and Pete* story, *Bill and Pete Go Down the Nile*. Brainstorm possible ways Bill and Pete might come to the rescue in this story. List all student answers on a piece of chart paper or on a black or white board so you and your children can come back to them after reading the story.

- Looking at the front cover, who do you think the eyes belong to?
- Looking at the back of the book, name all of the characters.
- Bill's father died when he was made into a suitcase by the Bad Guy. Who could this other crocodile be?

Vocabulary

There are some vocabulary words to look up, just like in the first story about Bill and Pete. Use the dictionary and also an atlas to locate the following words and places:

stowaways

Louisiana

bayou

levee

READING THE STORY

Read the story with the children, pausing to discuss the illustrations as you go along. Tomie dePaola inserts many details specific to New Orleans and the bayou in this story but does not actually refer to them in the text. Discussing the illustrations will bring additional richness and understanding of the setting of the story.

THINKING CRITICALLY ABOUT THE TEXT

- Why do Bill and Pete take on the project of finding little Jane Allison?
- Bill and Pete take their backpacks along for the journey. What do you think might be inside them?

- What does it mean to become a stowaway? Do you think it's possible that a crocodile could actually stow away on an ocean liner and hide among the luggage? How about a bird?
- What do we learn about ocean liners from the illustrations Tomie dePaola has drawn?
- What words would you use to describe the Rich Lady? Bad Guy's Big Bad Brother?
- What do crocodiles eat? Do they really eat bananas? If you don't know what they eat, where could you find out?
- Describe some differences between the Louisiana bayou and the Nile River? You might need to look at copies of *Bill and Pete* and *Bill and Pete Go Down the Nile* to find some of the answers.
- Using the illustrations to explain your answers, describe the Bad Guy's Big Bad Brother's Exotic Animal Farm.
- Does anything surprising happen in the story?

SHARING PERSONAL EXPERIENCES

- Have you ever been on a boat or a cruise? What was it like to be on the water?
- Have you ever seen any of the exotic animals illustrated in the book? Where?

RESPONDING TO THE TEXT: INTEGRATED LANGUAGE ARTS—REFERENCE SKILLS

Using atlases or world maps, have children trace the path that an ocean liner might take to get from the Nile River in Egypt to the Mississippi River.

- What bodies of water might they cruise through?
- Is there more than one possible route?
- How long do you think it takes for the ocean liner to get from the Nile River in Egypt to Louisiana in the story?
- How long might it take today?
- What would be the most direct route?

Using maps and information from the Internet or from a friendly travel agent, see if you can find the answers.

Researching Endangered Species

Many of the animals that are in cages in the Bad Guy's Big Bad Brother's Exotic Animal Farm are endangered. Using an encyclopedia or the Internet (with guidance and permission, of course!), learn about some of the animals that are endangered in our world. What animal would you like to rescue from becoming extinct? Write about the animal, draw or sketch a picture of it, and share that information with your classmates.

RESPONDING TO THE TEXT: WRITING

Rescue Attempts

Have you ever attempted to rescue something? Perhaps you tried to save a bug, a worm, or an animal of some kind? Share your attempt in a story entitled, "[Your name]'s Amazing Rescue! If children have not rescued or saved something, have each one make up a creative story including an animal that he or she might like to save. What animal or being would each child save and how would they do it?

Love Notes in a Bottle

Have children write a note to their parents and insert them into small, plastic soda bottles. These can be presented as a gift to the parents if children insert other little items into the bottles as well. A fun gift might be to put the note into a bottle filled with a little powdered bubble bath. The bottle floats in the tub and the bubble bath can be used by a tired mom looking for a leisurely soak—a nice Mother's Day gift idea.

Writing a News Flash

Children write the news bulletin that might air on the radio or television after the Bad Guy's Big Bad Brother is caught. What might an announcer say? Can children be short and specific about the announcement? Give children a pretend microphone and have them share the news flash announcements with each other.

RESPONDING TO THE TEXT: ART

Note: These activities can be used after reading *Bill and Pete, Bill and Pete Go Down the Nile,* and *Bill and Pete to the Rescue.*

Create a Mural of the Nile River Area or One of New Orleans

Use paint, paper collage, or other art techniques to design and create a mural based on the information children discover from their research. It helps to have children draw a plan first. It might be fun to include characters from the book such as Bill and Pete, the Bad Guy, the Rich Lady, or the Bad Guy's Big Bad Brother.

Self-portraits

Children design self-portraits of themselves as a good friend in the coming year.

- Children can have a friend trace their body onto butcher paper and then paint or color their images. (A variation of this is for children to make a back and front, use newspaper to "stuff them," and staple the outer edges to make three-dimensional self-portraits.)
- They can paint, sketch, or draw themselves on any size paper, either by themselves or with a friend
- They can be given the same size piece of paper as everyone else in the class but be given freedom to depict themselves artistically in their own way. These portraits could be displayed around the room or next to their names if you do the Art response activity from *Andy, That's My Name*.
- They can make a figure of themselves out of tag board and use fabric to clothe themselves in a favorite outfit. Children love working with fabric and trims!

Make "Wanted" Posters

Have children design "Wanted, a good friend!" posters of themselves (like those you might see at the post office, only nicer!) Try this as a class exercise first, using the character of Bill or Pete so children will have a model of what to do.

The posters could include the following information:

- a picture of themselves (either a photo or a drawing)
- name
- height
- hair and eye color
- clothing last seen in
- favorite hobbies or food
- can often be found in/at . . .
- identifying traits
- anything else your children would like to add

An example might look like this:

WANTED

Name: _____
Height: _____
Weight: _____
Hair Color: _____
Eye Color: _____

Can be found: _____
_____
_____

Special Talents: _____
_____
_____

Make a "Wanted" Poster for the Bad Guy or His Big Bad Brother

Return to the *Bill and Pete* books to look at the identifying features of the Bad Guy or the Bad Guy's Big Bad Brother.

A "Wanted" poster for a villain often includes the following:

a picture of the villain, including a profile	distinguishing characteristics
height	a nickname
weight	what he or she is known for
hair color	method of escape
eye color	helpful clues
where last seen	a reward
the crime committed	

These poster ideas are adapted from a section on literary posters in Terry Johnson and Daphne Louis's book, *Literacy through Literature*. Johnson explains the concept of "Wanted" and "Missing Person" posters more thoroughly and gives examples to use with your students.

❤❤❤ — ❤❤❤ — ❤❤❤ — ❤❤❤ — ❤❤❤ — ❤❤❤

Chapter 5

A Visit with Tomie dePaola

This literary guide was created to complement the video *A Visit with Tomie dePaola* and to assist teachers and librarians in celebrating Tomie dePaola in every elementary classroom and library. For information on ordering the video, see the bibliography at the end of the book.

BACKGROUND

Children, teachers, and librarians all over the world have fallen in love with the works of Tomie dePaola, one of America's most popular children's illustrators and authors of our time. They are constantly sending him letters (over 100,000 received each year) asking personal questions such as:

- What is your favorite food?
- Where do you live?
- Do you have any pets?
- Where do you get the ideas for your books?
- How did you learn how to draw, and how can I learn how to draw and write like you?

The questions are as varied as the children, teachers, and librarians who send them. The video, produced by Tomie dePaola himself, not only welcomes us into his home and studio, but it also helps answer many questions in the minds of curious children and educators!

SUMMARY

The video begins with Tomie welcoming us into his home in New Hampshire. We walk right into Tomie's living room and immediately feel at home with him. Tomie shares his love for folk art, part of his heart collection, and how he treats his white walls as if they were pieces of paper or canvas. He takes us into his kitchen, where he shares his passion for cooking and also a personal story about cooking from his childhood. We then visit the beautiful gardens he has designed, where he says, "being an artist, color and beauty are a very important part of my life." Taking a short walk across his courtyard, Tomie then takes us into his 200-year-old barn and studio. We learn about his fine art painting as he shares with us a work in progress and several different examples of his recent painting and folk art projects. We visit his archival collections, both books and paintings carefully stored in other parts of the barn.

Finally we go to his illustration studio where Tomie shares the history of his most famous character, Strega Nona, and draws his beloved Italian grandmother witch step by step. As we learn more about where Tomie gets his ideas, his trademark heart, and his love for drawing and painting, and we hear some advice for young readers and writers, we have the great fortune of viewing video clips from his childhood. The video concludes with Tomie dePaola drawing himself as a child and sharing his hopes that his books bring joy and laughter into the lives of those who read them. Tomie concludes the video by saying that he hopes "young people experience life as just a wonderful, wonderful thing . . . and I hope my books help do that."

HOW TO USE THIS LITERARY GUIDE

Many teachers and librarians already do an author study about Tomie dePaola. The video is a wonderful way of learning first-hand about Tomie dePaola from the man himself. Many teachers have been looking for additional ways to introduce Tomie dePaola to their students and to celebrate him and the literature he has created. This literary guide will do just that. It also will also give you:

- section-by-section specifics about the video for those who are interested in knowing more about Tomie's house and studio
- activities that will teach you more about your students as you learn more about Tomie dePaola
- many activities to pick and choose from so the way you celebrate the literature of Tomie dePaola fits into your teaching style and time schedule
- ways to celebrate Tomie dePaola's birthday or create your own
- a Tomie dePaola celebration in your classroom, library, and school

PRE-VIEWING ACTIVITIES

Show copies of *Strega Nona, The Art Lesson,* and other Tomie dePaola books to your students. Do they know who the author of these books is? His name is pronounced "Tommy da-POW-la." Do they know any other stories that this author has illustrated or written? If so, your children may be ready to watch the video about Tomie dePaola. If not, spend some time just enjoying some of Tomie's books prior to watching the video. A suggestion might be to share Tomie's autobiographical stories with your children. They are listed below:

Autobiographical Books about Tomie dePaola

Andy, That's My Name, The Art Lesson, The Baby Sister, Nana Upstairs & Nana Downstairs, Now One Foot, Now the Other, Oliver Button Is a Sissy, Tom, and *Watch Out for the Chicken Feet in Your Soup.*

Other Books by Tomie dePaola

You could also take the time to share other books by Tomie from a variety of genres. These are just some of them:

Fiction: The *Strega Nona* Stories, *Bill and Pete, Bill and Pete Go Down the Nile, Bill and Pete to the Rescue, Alice Nizzy Nazzy: The Witch of Santa Fe, The Barkers* series.

Nonfiction/informational: *The Popcorn Book, The Kids' Cat Book, The Quicksand Book, The Cloud Book.*

Legends: *The Legend of the Bluebonnet, The Legend of the Indian Paintbrush, The Legend of the Poinsettia.*

Holiday Books: *Country Angel Christmas, The Night before Christmas, Merry Christmas, Strega Nona, The Family Christmas Tree Book, The Vanishing Pumpkin, The Spooky Halloween Party.*

Collections: *Tomie dePaola's Mother Goose, Tomie dePaola's Book of Poems, Tomie dePaola's Favorite Nursery Tales.*

Any of your personal favorites! There are now more than 220 books illustrated by Tomie dePaola so check your school library's collection.

FOLLOW-UP DISCUSSION

Take time to have some follow-up discussion, asking questions such as:

- What do you notice about the illustrations Tomie dePaola draws?
- What do you like about his books?
- Who are some of your favorite characters?

FIND NEW HAMPSHIRE AND CONNECTICUT ON A MAP

Tomie lives in a small village in New Hampshire. Help children find the state of New Hampshire on a map. Tell them Tomie lives about an hour and a half from Boston (point out Boston, MA). He is also close to New York so he can go visit his publishers when he needs to.

Now have children find Connecticut on the map. Tomie's home town is Meriden, Connecticut. See if you can find Meriden on a map of the state of Connecticut. Meriden was a silver mining town in the late 1800s.

CREATING A K-W-L

To activate prior knowledge and to find out what children already know about Tomie dePaola, brainstorm and list all of those things children know or think they know on a K-W-L (**K**now-**W**ant to learn-**L**earned) chart. (See K-W-L example in Chapter 3, p. 87.) List younger children's ideas on chart paper or newsprint. Have older children write what they already know on sentence strips and attach them to a chart. Display the chart where children can add to it in the future.

Look through some of Tomie dePaola's many books and ask children what questions they have about Tomie dePaola. What would they like to learn more about? Write those questions down in the column, *What we want to learn*. Return to this chart later after watching the video. Leave room for children to add new facts or information if they have the chance to view the video again later or gain new information from some of his books.

MAKING PREDICTIONS

Show the front cover of the video to the children and have them make predictions about where Tomie dePaola lives and works. Below are just a few ideas to spark the imagination of you and the children you teach.

- What do you think Tomie dePaola's house will look like on the inside?
- What kinds of things do you think Tomie dePaola collects?
- Do you think Tomie dePaola has any pets? If so, what kinds?
- What do you think are some of Tomie dePaola's favorite things to do?
- Where do you suppose Tomie dePaola does his illustrations? How many books do you think he has illustrated?
- Where do you think Tomie dePaola gets his ideas?

WATCHING THE VIDEO

The video is about thirty minutes long. It can be viewed at length or divided into sections for viewing. If you choose to view it in sections, the following are natural stopping points for discussion:

- Tomie takes us into his living room, or "Great Room," into the kitchen, and then into the gardens (pause for discussion).
- Tomie takes us in his barn, where we learn about the fine art work he does, see some recent painting and folk art projects, and view parts of his archival collections (pause for discussion).
- Tomie takes us to his drawing table in his studio, where he draws and tells us about the creation of Strega Nona, shares his love for drawing and painting, tells us where his ideas come from, and talks about the importance of hard work and creating your own work and not "copying." He also shares his hopes for children.

A VISIT WITH TOMIE DEPAOLA: A SECTION-BY-SECTION LOOK AT THE VIDEO

This section will answer more specific wonderings in the minds of curious librarians, teachers, and children. Hopefully, the information below, some of which also appears on Tomie dePaola's Web page www.Tomie.com, will answer some of the specific questions people may have about the video. I have also provided some of Tomie dePaola's quotes throughout the video.

Greetings Tomie!

Tomie dePaola greets us at the front door of his house. He invites us into the entryway of his Yankee barn-style home. Immediately you will begin to see some of Tomie's collections—the black birds, hats, folk art, and so on. Notice the heart pin that Tomie is wearing? The heart is his trademark, and he has a wonderful heart collection that you will soon see.

The Great Room

Next we go into Tomie's living room, or what his friends call the "Great Room." It is painted all white because Tomie loves the color white. "I treat them [the walls] like they are a piece of paper or canvas. I put things against them and arrange and rearrange those things," he says.

"I have lots and lots of folk art," Tomie says. "I love folk art and collect it." We see some black crows done by Navajo artists and lots of other Mexican folk art.

Notice the heart collection on the table. The heart-shaped maple sugar mold was given to Tomie on his fiftieth birthday by friends Nancy, Jill, and Steve. In *The Quilt Story,* Tomie dedicated the illustrations to Nancy and her daughter, Jill, and Jill and Steve's daughter, Becca.

When Tomie is showing the heart-shaped sugar mold, notice the square object in the corner in back of him against the wall. Those are the alphabet blocks from his childhood that you will also see in the book *Now One Foot, Now the Other.* Tomie often uses the blocks to spell messages of greetings to his guests who visit.

The painting of the young man in the blue shirt is a self-portrait Tomie painted in 1956 when he was a senior at Pratt Institute.

Tomie loves folk art. You will see it everywhere you look. The "pincushion-like" folk art bird was done by an artist friend, Kelly Buntin-Johnson, from Kansas City, Missouri. Tomie really likes her artwork. He also has a jacket and other artwork done by Kelly.

The angel paintings on either side of the opening were done by Tomie.

The letter boxes that spell "Tomie" were a gift from Bob Hechtel, Tomie's assistant. Inside each box is a message that a donation had been made to a charity in his name.

The Native American paintings were ones that Tomie painted. The drawings were done in 1976. They were put in a drawer until 1978, when he painted them.

Above the mantel is a painting of Mary and child that Tomie did in 1958. Between the crows on the table are a plate and an ear of corn that Tomie painted. The Great Room looks out onto Tomie's deck and gardens. It also looks into the kitchen where we go and visit with Tomie next.

The Kitchen

Tomie loves to cook and he tries to cook for himself every day (when he's not traveling!). He is preparing one of his favorite dishes: pasta with a sauce made of leeks, fennel, Belgian endive, and garlic. Tomie loves to have big parties and entertain guests.

Tomie tells a story about growing up and being able to do one thing you really want to do on your birthday. On his fifth birthday he chose to make his own supper: a "Popeye" (directions provided on p. 127). Tomie still has the original pan he made his Popeye in. It has a special place of honor hanging on his kitchen wall.

Tomie hangs his pots and pans just like he hangs his pictures. He also decorates his counters. You will notice that everything is arranged beautifully in his kitchen, from the spices hanging on the wall to everything on the counters too!

The Gardens

Tomie loves flowers. He says, "Being an artist, color and beauty are a very important part of my life." These gardens are seen in early June. There are still some tulips blooming, as well as different types of lilies. During the summer, many annuals are planted around Tomie's gardens. Some of his favorites are geraniums, marigolds, zinnias, and petunias.

The whitebird weathervane (the whitebird is also one of Tomie's familiar symbols) was also designed by Tomie. In the filming of the video, Tomie and Bob saw it move for the first time!

Across the Courtyard to the Barn

Tomie leaves his house to "commute" to work every day. He designed the New Hampshire cobbled courtyard to reflect some of his Italian heritage. Tomie is half Italian and half Irish.

The barn is a 200-year-old building that has three floors. There are five dogs that are loose inside and love to jump up on visitors. Four are Welsh terriers: Madison, Moffat, Morgan, and Markus. One is an Airedale terrier named Bingley Too, and he belonged to Bob Hechtel, Tomie's assistant. Madison was so named because he was born in a car as it was entering Madison County. Moffat and Morgan were named after characters in *The Corn Is Green*. Markus was adopted. His full name in Markus Barkus. His nickname is "Barky." Can you guess why?

Tomie no longer has cats but he has had many over the years. He used to have two Abyssinian cats named Foshay (named after the Foshay Tower in Minneapolis) and Dayton (named after the department store in Minneapolis). Erik (Satie) was the Abysinnian cat that Tomie had for the longest time. He lived to be seventeen years old. Tomie also had a cat named Bomba (named after Bomba, the Jungle Boy) who was an Ocicat. You will see many of Tomie's cats and dogs in his picture books.

On the desk you will see pictures of Tomie with his sister, Maureen. The book *The Baby Sister* is about Maureen.

Tomie's paints and paintbrushes are always very organized and displayed artistically, like the artwork or collections in other parts of his home.

Once again, Tomie talks about how important it is for him and how fortunate he is to work in a "beautiful, beautiful space. Every artist has a studio. I'm lucky to have such a big one."

We see one of Tomie's recent fine art paintings. "I get ideas for some of my books from doing paintings." When Tomie prepares a canvas for painting he puts gesso on it. Gesso is a plaster of Paris-type substance prepared with glue that is brushed on canvas to make it more absorbent of paint.

We see some of his triptychs and diptychs he is preparing for a one-man art show. While Tomie is discussing the application of gesso, in the background on the bottom shelf, you can (with a careful eye) make out two large stars. They are the stars that were put on the doors to Tomie's dressing rooms when he taped episodes of *Barney and Friends*. Tomie dePaola was the first artist/illustrator to be invited onto the *Barney and Friends* show.

Tomie loves Mexican folk art. The large painting of the Mexican dinner he painted is called *Frida's Table*, inspired by Frida Kahlo, a famous Mexican artist. It is done from a bird's-eye view. Tomie imagined that he was above the table looking down on it, in order to paint everything on the table.

Notice the shrines inspired by a friend's gift, "Our Saints of the Dashboard." Tomie loved the idea of shrines and "found object boxes" so much that he bought his own wooden boxes to paint and create. He painted the edges of the boxes and has added beans, peas, flowers, candles, and other things to make his own found object boxes. (Directions for these are on p. 122).

"Warm-up paintings" are what Tomie calls the small, almost postage stamp-sized pictures he does when he needs to warm up his hand and wrist before doing a lot of artwork and especially after doing lots of autographing. He has framed these warm-up paintings for an art show.

And of course, we see many Tomie dePaola books all around. There are "always books everywhere," says Tomie.

The Archival Collections

On the second floor of the barn, the books and illustrations of Tomie's archival collections are carefully stored. An archival collection of this type is the careful preservation of every book or illustration someone has done so that it is documented for history. Tomie shows us his special bookcases where a copy of every single book he has written and/or illustrated is stored. He also has different editions that have been published, such as books translated into other languages. You will notice some leather editions of several books. These are special gifts presented to Tomie by his publisher, G. P. Putnam's Sons.

Pieces of Tomie's original artwork are stored in gray metal files, using acid-free paper. Acid-free paper is used to preserve artwork, photographs, and other artifacts to keep them from fading and deteriorating. Tomie has tried to save at least one illustration from each book he has done. We see original artwork from *The Legend of Old Befana, Tom, Strega Nona's Magic Lessons,* and *The Night before Christmas* (Tomie's one-hundredth illustrated book, done in 1980.)

The popcorn machine was given to Tomie by his publisher, G. P. Putnam's Sons, on Tomie's fifty-first birthday. Tomie's favorite snack is popcorn. Be sure to check out *The Popcorn Book,* a popular Tomie dePaola book.

Tomie's Illustration Studio

Tomie draws Strega Nona for us as he tells about her creation. Strega Nona is an original character that Tomie created as he was doodling (everyone thought he was taking meticulous notes!) during a staff meeting at the college where he was teaching (now known as Colby-Sawyer College). The sketch remained on his wall for some time until the idea of Strega Nona came to him. Tomie's inspiration for the Strega Nona stories came from stories such as "The Magic Porridge Pot" and "The Sorcerer's Apprentice." Of course, she was also inspired by his Italian heritage and thus, was put in an Italian setting.

Tomie always begins to draw Strega Nona by drawing her kerchief, saying that "it makes me feel comfortable . . . , if I get the kerchief right, then I know I can get her face right." Have you noticed that Tomie likes to wear kerchiefs (bandannas) himself?

Tomie shares his love of painting. In this painting of Strega Nona he is using lots of water. "I learned along the way first from art school and then from doing lots and lots of books that I learn as I do things," he says. "It's the same for learning how to cook, draw, write books and tap dance. I tap danced for a long, long time!"

We see teenagers Carol Morrissey and Tomie dance as "Señior and Señiorita Swing" (thanks to Tomie's family home movies). At Tomie's sixtieth birthday party, Carol and Tomie surprised the 400 guests in attendance with an impromptu dance number!

Tomie draws a very special apron on Strega Nona—one with his trademark heart on it. He also signs his name, including a heart inside the letter "T" of his name.

He says, "I don't know if you can tell, but I am so happy when I'm sitting here at my drawing table painting. I love to watch the way the colors come together and land on the paper."

Back in Tomie's Living Room (the Great Room)

"I love books," Tomie says. "I can't imagine not loving reading. I like to tell my young friends, 'If you can read, you can learn everything about anything and anything about everything'.

"If you want to be a writer, you have to read and you have to read everything you can. Because that's how you learn about writing, oddly enough. And then, once you've read enough and feel confident that you, too, can tell a story, then you also have to practice! And you have to be willing to do it over and over and over again.

"Whenever I write a story, I know that the first draft is not going to be the way the story turns out when it's published in a book. And a lot of young people don't like to do that. They don't like to do it over again. But, if you want to be a writer, you better get used to it because you're going to have to."

Tomie tells us about his twin cousins who are both artists. We see Franny and Fuffy, walking with little Tomie in the foreground of a home video. Franny and Fuffy's mother, Tomie's brother Joe, and Tomie's father are sending the twins off to art school. Franny and Fuffy are the twin cousins who are mentioned in *The Art Lesson*. They give Tomie two very important pieces of advice for becoming an artist that Tomie still remembers: "*real* artists don't copy and you must practice, practice, practice!"

What Tomie thinks that what they meant by "real artists don't copy" is that "you don't look at and copy someone else's idea. You really try to see and do something for yourself."

The first book Tomie did that involved family memories was *Nana Upstairs & Nana Downstairs*. It is about his Irish great-grandmother and grandmother when Tomie was four years old. It is still in print and was twenty-five years old in 1998. Tomie released a full-color version of *Nana Upstairs & Nana Downstairs* at that time, which was his two-hundredth illustrated book! The book deals sensitively with serious issues of love and loss. It took a lot of courage for Tomie to write about such a serious subject.

In a dream (actually a nightmare) Tomie had after finishing *Nana Upstairs & Nana Downstairs,* his Italian grandmother (Nana Fall-River) calls him over to her porch, saying to him, "Hey, my friend [her nickname for him], come here! How come you no write a book about me!?" Tomie woke up and told her, "I will Nana, I will!" Thus, *Watch Out for the Chicken Feet in Your Soup* was written and illustrated about his Italian grandmother. It became Tomie's second autobiographical book.

Tomie dePaola says, "I never know where I'm going to get inspired, but my family has given me lots of ideas for stories. The more I think about them, the more ideas I get these days."

Tomie's father had a movie camera when Tomie was just a little boy, so in the video we see a picture of Baby Tomie with his mother on the front porch of their home.

In the next family picture, the family is eating spaghetti. Tomie's mother is at the left and Nana Fall River is next to her. The others at the table are Italian aunts, uncles, and cousins. Tomie says that everyone's just "piling in the spaghetti! I suppose that's what inspired Big Anthony!"

As Tomie talks about his "crazy" relatives, we see one of them doing a somersault in the yard. We then see young Tomie showing off on the rings in his yard.

When people visit Tomie, they comment that the rooms look like some of the pages in his books. He says, "Of course. They should, for I draw the way I live."

Tomie talks about Ben Shahn, who was a famous contemporary artist and teacher at a summer art school in Maine, who said, "It's not only the way you draw and paint, but, it's the way you live that makes you an artist."

Tomie's Illustration Studio

Tomie says that he has a strong work ethic. This is due to his parents, his art teachers, and definitely all of his editors. But, he says, "I try to make the hard work not show."

As Tomie paints a picture of himself as a child, he tells us that there used to be a "grown-up" painter named Henri Matisse who said that "when people looked at his paintings, he wanted them to feel as comfortable as though they were sitting in a big armchair." He didn't want them to know about all the hard work that went on, but to enjoy what he finally created. Tomie has that same desire for those who read and enjoy his books. "I don't want my viewers to see all of the hard work, but the hard work is certainly there."

"I want them to feel as comfortable as if they were sitting in a cozy armchair. I want people to laugh, and some [of my books] also make people cry. I always want there to be a sense of joy and a sense of hope, that life is really wonderful and life is really worth living. My hope, for young people especially, is that life is just a wonderful, wonderful thing to experience, and I hope my books help do that."

RESPONDING TO THE VIDEO

There are many ways for children to respond to the texts and videos that can demonstrate their understanding and comprehension of them. Below are some ideas to spark responses that you and your children may choose to do in response to viewing *A Visit with Tomie dePaola*.

FOLLOW-UP SHARED DISCUSSION ABOUT THE VIDEO

Return to the K-W-L

- What are some of the things we learned about Tomie dePaola?

If your students are younger, record right on the K-W-L chart itself. Have older children write something they learned on a sentence strip. Give them time to share what they have learned with each other prior to attaching it to the K-W-L chart.

Note: You may need additional chart paper to enlarge your chart as children may remember more facts about Tomie dePaola than you have room for on your original chart. If you run out of room, you could ask children with additional information to write their new fact about Tomie dePaola on a heart-shaped piece of paper to create a border for your K-W-L.

Additional Questions for Discussion

- Were any of our predictions right about Tomie dePaola? (Go back to the list of predictions children made if you happened to write them down.)
- Were some of the questions on our K-W- L chart answered? If not, where do you think we could find additional information about Tomie dePaola?
- What did you learn about Tomie dePaola that surprised or delighted you?

RESPONDING TO THE VIDEO: ART

Create Warm-up Drawings and Paintings

Distribute small pieces (even miniature scraps) of art paper for children to sketch freely, draw, or paint on. They could use these for a time of "art drafting," to clarify their plans for future drawing and art projects, or as the project itself. Remind children that Tomie dePaola used these as a way of warming up his wrist and arm to get ready for other artwork he was going to work on. Children may want to matte these small drawings with large construction paper borders. For a special project, see if a local framing store will give you leftover scraps of matte board or sell them inexpensively and help children matte their creations. You don't have to cut the matte board. Children's artwork can be glued directly onto a piece of matte board or construction paper with wonderful effects.

Drawing from a Bird's Eye View

Tomie dePaola's enormous painting *Frida's Table* shows a Mexican dinner from a bird's eye view looking downward. Have children draw or paint something from a bird's eye view, imagining they are looking down from a low-flying airplane.

Suggestions might be

- their favorite dinner or meal
- their bedroom or a room in their house
- the classroom or library
- their favorite place to play or the school playground
- a park

Paint Diptychs or Triptychs

Have children plan out and paint their own diptychs—two paintings together—or triptychs—three paintings together. Tomie dePaola used Mexican folk art for his inspiration. Use Mexican folk art or some of the artists you are currently studying as inspiration for your children's artwork. Have the artwork matted to share with others.

Found Object Boxes and Shrines

For this project you might want to watch the section of the video that shows the shrine that Tomie was given and the shrines and found object boxes that Tomie made. According to the *Webster's Dictionary,* a shrine is "any place or object hallowed by its history or associations." There are a lot of shrines depicted through Mexican folk art. Children can make their own personal shrines or found object boxes. (You can select the term you are comfortable using.) These do not have to have a religious connotation, but can simply include objects that are significant to a child or just items that he or she likes.

You will need

- small wooden or heavy cardboard boxes. Collect or make small wooden or cardboard boxes for this activity. You might send a note home to parents several months in advance of this project, asking them to watch for and collect small boxes. You may have a handy parent who is willing to cut small thin pieces of wood for your children to glue together.
- project glue or wood glue
- paint appropriate to the wood or cardboard
- small objects that children gather—favorite personal trinkets or artifacts, seeds, pods, and various small objects from nature; or collections of objects

Procedures

Have children design and then sketch their found object box. Encourage children to first choose whether to do a personal or natural found object box and then bring in the objects they will use to assist them in the designing process.

Considerations for children to think about in designing and sketching:

- How will they position their box—horizontally or vertically?
- How will they paint the outside of the box? Will they use a pattern on some of the outside edges like Tomie dePaola did, or will they draw some personal favorites?

If the box is related to nature, children might want to look at some of the patterns and designs that naturally occur in nature for inspiration.

- What will they use on the inside of their box? Will they use paint, fabric, wallpaper or something else?
- How will they arrange the objects within and outside of their box?
- What will they use to keep the objects in place?

When children have gone through the designing and sketching phase, give them ample time to work on these. You might want children to share their plans as a whole class in order to find those who can work together and share materials. It also may be convenient to set up several work stations or centers in the classroom where children can work in small groups. Younger children may need adult assistance so you will need to plan around the parent and classroom volunteers you have.

When children have created their found object boxes, ask them:

- Have you named your piece of artwork and signed it?
- How will you share your artwork? Will you put it on display and write a short description of it?

Chapter 6

Celebrating Tomie dePaola

There are as many ways to celebrate the literature of Tomie dePaola as your imagination will allow—at least as many as the number of books Tomie has illustrated (more than 220!). Pick and choose from some of the activities below, and add them to your own ideas to create your own Tomie dePaola Celebration.

Introduce Tomie dePaola

Consider using Tomie dePaola as your first author study of the year since Tomie's birthday is at the beginning of the school year, on September 15. Use the month of September to get to know your students as you get to know this wonderful author. Many of the ideas shared in the autobiographical chapter of this book are very appropriate to begin with.

Create an Author Study

Of course, you don't have to begin the year with a Tomie dePaola unit! Using your present curriculum, plan an author study that will meet the needs of you and your class. Use any of the above activities and weave some of those that follow in this literary guide with your own great ideas.

Celebrate Tomie dePaola Day

You can do this on September 15, or on the fifteenth of any month read Tomie dePaola books and do special activities with them. In *The Art Lesson,* we learn about Tomie's first days of school and especially his first "official" art lesson. Share the story and do some of the crayon art activities children love to do. You will find a list of possibilities in the Art response section later in this guide. Make sure you share *your* favorite Tomie dePaola books!

CELEBRATING TOMIE DEPAOLA: INTEGRATED LANGUAGE ARTS

Some of "My Favorite Things"

In the video *A Visit with Tomie dePaola,* Tomie invites us into his house and studio, where we learn about many of his favorite things to do and to collect. Have children write and talk about some of their favorites: activities, collections, hobbies. You could even invite children to make individual tag board displays or a group bulletin board display of their favorites in order to share them with others. This is a great activity to do at the beginning of the year.

CELEBRATING TOMIE DEPAOLA: WRITING

Send Tomie dePaola a Birthday Card from the Class

Have your children draw or paint their original creations and send them to Tomie for his birthday (September 15) or half-birthday (March 15th). Cards can be sent to:

Tomie dePaola
Penguin Young Reader's Group
345 Hudson Street
New York, NY

Writing Personal Stories

Tomie dePaola likes to share stories and videos from his childhood. Encourage children to write short stories about themselves. Have them look through family pictures or home videotapes (with parental assistance) and write about an event they think is exciting or memorable. Encourage children who are older to go through the process of writing a draft, revising it, and editing it until it is finalized. Remind them of Tomie's advice in the video *A Visit with Tomie dePaola*: "If you want to be a writer, you better get used to it [revising, or doing it over again] because you have to." When children have completed their personal stories, have them share their photos (or videos) before sharing their written stories.

CELEBRATING TOMIE DEPAOLA: COOKING AND LITERATURE RESPONSES

Make Popcorn, Tomie's Favorite Food!

Follow the recipes at the end of Tomie dePaola's delightful *The Popcorn Book* or have children share their family's favorite way (or brand) of making popcorn. Other popcorn ideas include making picture collages with popcorn, researching the history of popcorn, making popcorn balls, creating popcorn creatures, estimating how many kernels are in a little jar of popcorn, graphing children's favorite popcorn flavor, and comparing different types of popcorn. Find these and other popcorn math ideas in the "Popcorn Math" chapter of *Box It or Bag It Math,* by Donna Burke, Allyn Snider, and Paula Symonds.

Make Potatoes (*Jamie O'Rourke and the Big Potato*)

Have children share their family's favorite way of preparing potatoes. If possible, take time to bake potatoes and use favorite toppings. See more ideas in Chapter 3 of this book. Also see Chapter 7 in *Box It or Bag It Math* for math ideas.

Make Bread (*Tony's Bread* and *Watch out for the Chicken Feet in Your Soup*)

After reading *Tony's Bread*, children could taste or make *panettone* or another type of bread. It's magical for children to see how bread rises and to compare the bread before and after it's baked. After reading *Watch out for the Chicken Feet in Your Soup*, children could make bread dolls at school, if permitted, or you could send a copy of the recipe home for children to make them with their parents.

Make Pasta (The *Strega Nona* Stories)

There are many ways for children to make and enjoy pasta. Adding some boiling water to ramen noodles can be done quite successfully in school. You can also make homemade pasta and cut it by hand or bring in a pasta machine for your pasta party. A good recipe can be found in *The Kids' Multicultural Cookbook,* by Deanna Cook.

Make Pancakes (*Pancakes for Breakfast*)

Make pancakes using the recipe included in this wonderful, wordless book or have children bring in their family favorites. Children can also bring in their familys' favorite pancake recipes, and a parent or volunteer can type them up and compile a class recipe book to share with students' families.

Make Cookies (*Jingle, the Christmas Clown* and all Tomie dePaola Books)

Use the recipe for Donna Chiara's Stelline d'Oro given at the end of *Jingle, the Christmas Clown* or your favorite recipe for cookies. Use star cookie cutters for the Stelline d'Oro or heart and dove cookie cutters to celebrate some of Tomie dePaola's trademark symbols found in most of his books.

Make an Official Tomie dePaola "Popeye!" (from *A Visit with Tomie dePaola*)

Recipe follows.

CELEBRATING TOMIE DEPAOLA: ART

Crayon Art Ideas (*The Art Lesson*)

Some possible ideas are:

- Free drawing anything children want to draw.
- Crayon resist artwork using watercolors over crayons.
- Try watercolor pencils or crayons! Watercolor crayons are wonderful if you haven't discovered them yet. I have my children draw pictures with an ultra-fine Sharpie pen and then fill in the drawings using watercolor crayons. They are always a success.
- Crayon shavings ironed in between waxed paper is a favorite if you have an assistant to help with the iron.

Tomie's Popeye Recipe

You will need:

- ♥ a small frying pan – Tomie's is a little cast iron frying pan, but any kind will do
- ♥ 1 to 2 teaspoons butter or margarine
- ♥ a small circular cookie or biscuit cutter about 2 inches wide
- ♥ one piece of bread
- ♥ one egg
- ♥ a parent or older person to help you fry

1. Cut a hole in the middle of a piece of bread with the cookie or biscuit cutter. Set aside the round piece of bread.
2. Melt some butter or margarine in a small frying pan. When the butter is melted, fry one side of the bread hole and one side of the piece of bread for about one minute. Tomie told me that he used to fry the hole first, in "lots of butter," when he was a child!
3. Crack an egg into the center of the hole in the piece of bread. Sprinkle with salt and pepper if desired.
4. Cook 2 to 3 minutes more, until the egg is just set and the bread is beginning to turn golden brown.
5. Gently flip the pieces of bread and egg over with a spatula and cook another 1 to 2 minutes depending on how you like your eggs.
6. When cooked to your liking, use a spatula to take out the piece of bread and egg and place it on your plate.
7. Place the small fried hole on top of the egg and enjoy your "Popeye!"

♥ ♥ ♥

- Crayon etchings. Children use bright-colored crayons, then color with heavy, black crayon over them. Finally, they etch out a picture using a paper clip, bobby pin, or end of a paintbrush.

You will find additional art ideas in Chapter 5 of this book.

Heart Activities

Use Tomie's trademark symbol, the heart, for any number of creations. Some ideas are:

Use heart-shaped cookie cutters:

- to bake cookies.
- for baked or unbaked claydough creations.
- to create heart-shaped potato prints. Use the cookie cutter to stamp the cut side of a potato and then using a dull knife (pumpkin carving knives work great!) cut away the remaining potato revealing the heart shape. Use the stamp to create book covers, wrapping paper, and other decorative paper items.
- to compare sizes and perimeter if you collect a variety of different heart-shaped cutters.

Use heart-shaped sponges and erasers for printing booklet covers, wrapping paper, and mural designs.

Create a heart collection. Have your children bring in different items that are heart-shaped—tins, boxes, buttons, cards, and so forth. Gather children in a circle on the rug or around a table. Play 20 Questions, having children try to guess which heart-shaped item you or a designated child has chosen secretly. Explain that you will answer each guess or question using only a "yes" or "no" response. Encourage children to be specific in their questions about the item until they have either guessed which object you were thinking of or have asked twenty different questions.

Draw a heart-shaped still life. Arrange some of the heart-shaped items in a still life, if enough items were brought in, and have children sketch and paint them.

CELEBRATING TOMIE DEPAOLA: SCIENCE

Making Bubbles

Read *The Bubble Factory* and then have your children make their own "Wish Bubbles." Use them to blow bubbles and make wishes for Tomie on his birthday or for each child's classroom birthday celebration. Bubble mixtures and exploration activities can be found in *The Unbelievable Bubble Book,* by John Cassidy. Additional science activities can be found in *Bubblemania,* by Penny Raife Durant.

Note: When I was looking for a way to conclude my year with Kindergartners last year, I thought of a ritual for sending my children on to first grade. I read Tomie dePaola's *The Bubble Factory* in class toward the end of the school year. On the last day of school I gathered my children outside on a blanket, and we began thinking about our whole year and thanking each other for the wonderful times we had shared. Then I presented each child with their own bottle of "Wish Bubbles." We went around our circle and mentioned each child's name. After we named each child, we made a wish for that child for the coming year and blew bubbles to "make the wishes come true." It was a wonderful way to end the year with my children! The bubbles were a special treat!

Chapter 7

More Tomie dePaola Favorites

There are so many Tomie dePaola books to share with children! Here are some other favorite books I love to enjoy with the students in my classroom. For a complete listing of the books Tomie dePaola has written and illustrated, consult Tomie's Web site at www.Tomie.com.

Legends

The Legend of the Bluebonnet
The Legend of the Indian Paintbrush
The Legend of the Pointsettia

Nonfiction Books

The Cloud Book
The Kids' Cat Book
The Popcorn Book
The Quicksand Book

Christmas Books

The Clown of God (my own personal favorite)
Country Angel Christmas
An Early American Christmas
The Friendly Beasts
Jingle, the Christmas Clown
Miracle on 34th Street
The Night before Christmas

The *26 Fairmount Avenue* Series

26 Fairmount Avenue
Here We All Are

On My Way
Things Will NEVER Be the Same
What a Year

The *Barkers* Series

Meet the Barkers
A New Barker in the House
Trouble in the Barker's Class
Some early reader titles.

Religious Titles

Christopher, the Holy Giant
Francis, Poor Man of Assisi
The Holy Twins: Benedict and Scholastica
The Lady of Guadalupe
Mary, the Mother of Jesus
Pascual and the Kitchen Angels
Patrick, Patron Saint of Ireland

Bibliography

Ahlberg, Janet, and Allan Ahlberg. 1986. *The Jolly Postman or Other People's Letters.* Boston, MA: Little, Brown.
Bread Comes to Life: A Garden of Wheat and a Loaf to Eat. 2004. Produced by George Levenson. Berkeley, CA: Tricycle Press. Videocassette or DVD.
Bourgeois, Paulette. 1991. *The Amazing Potato Book.* Reading, MA: Addison-Wesley.
Brownlie, Faye, Susan Close, and Linda Wingren. 1990. *Tomorrow's Classroom Today: Strategies for Creating Active Readers, Writers, and Thinkers.* Portsmouth, NH: Heinemann.
Burke, Donna, Allyn Snider, and Paula Symonds. 1988. *Box It or Bag It Mathematics, Grades 1 and 2.* Portland, OR: Math Learning Center.
Carlson, Laurie. 1993. *ECOART! Earth-Friendly Art & Craft Experiences for 3–9-year-Olds.* Charlotte, VT: Williamson.
Cassidy, John. 1997. *The Unbelievable Bubble Book.* Palo Alto, CA: Klutz Press.
Charney, Ruth. 2002. *Teaching Children to Care: Classroom Management for Ethical and Academic Growth, K–8.* Greenfield, MA: Northeast Foundation for Children.
Child Development Project. 1996. *Ways We Want our Class to Be: Class Meetings That Build Commitment to Kindness and Learning.* Oakland, CA: Developmental Studies Center.
Cobb, Vicki, and Kathy Darling. 1983. *Bet You Can! Science Possibilities to Fool You.* New York: Avon.
Cobb, Vicki, and Kathy Darling. 1983. *Bet You Can't! Science Impossibilities to Fool You.* New York: Avon.
Cobb, Vicki, and Kathy Darling. 1993. *Wanna Bet? Science Challenges to Fool You.* New York: Avon.
Cook, Deanna. 1995. *Kids' Multicultural Cookbook.* Charlotte, VA: Kids Can!
Davies, Valentine. 1984. *Miracle on 34th Street.* Illustrated by Tomie dePaola. San Diego, CA: Harcourt Brace.
dePaola, Tomie. 1999. *26 Fairmount Avenue.* New York: G. P. Putnam's Sons.
dePaola, Tomie. 1973. *Andy, That's My Name.* New York: Simon & Schuster.
dePaola, Tomie. 1989. *The Art Lesson.* New York: G. P. Putnam's Sons.
dePaola, Tomie. 1996. *The Baby Sister.* New York: G. P. Putnam's Sons.
dePaola, Tomie. 1979. *Big Anthony and the Magic Ring.* San Diego, CA: Harcourt Brace.
dePaola, Tomie. 1998. *Big Anthony: His Story.* New York: G. P. Putnam's Sons.
dePaola, Tomie. 1978. *Bill and Pete.* New York: G. P. Putnam's Sons.
dePaola, Tomie. 1987. *Bill and Pete Go Down the Nile.* New York: G. P. Putnam's Sons.
dePaola, Tomie. 1998. *Bill and Pete to the Rescue.* New York: G. P. Putnam's Sons.
dePaola, Tomie. 1996. *The Bubble Factory.* New York: G. P. Putnam's Sons.
dePaola, Tomie. 1994. *Christopher, the Holy Giant.* New York: Holiday House.

dePaola, Tomie. 1975. *The Cloud Book*. New York: Holiday House.
dePaola, Tomie. 1978. *The Clown of God*. San Diego, CA: Harcourt Brace.
dePaola, Tomie. 1995. *Country Angel Christmas*. New York: G. P. Putnam's Sons.
dePaola, Tomie. 1987. *An Early American Christmas*. New York: Holiday House.
dePaola, Tomie. 1980. *The Family Christmas Tree Book*. New York: Holiday House.
dePaola, Tomie. 1982. *Francis, Poor Man of Assisi*. New York: Holiday House.
dePaola, Tomie. 1981. *The Friendly Beasts*. New York: G. P. Putnam's Sons.
dePaola, Tomie. 2000. *Here We All Are*. New York: G. P. Putnam's Sons.
dePaola, Tomie. 1992. *Jamie O'Rourke and the Big Potato*. New York: G. P. Putnam's Sons.
dePaola, Tomie. 2000. *Jamie O'Rourke and the Pooka*. New York: G. P. Putnam's Sons.
dePaola, Tomie. 1992. *Jingle, the Christmas Clown*. New York: G. P. Putnam's Sons.
dePaola, Tomie. 1979. *The Kids' Cat Book*. New York: Holiday House.
dePaola, Tomie. 1980. *The Lady of Guadalupe*. New York: Holiday House.
dePaola, Tomie. 1980. *The Legend of Old Befana*. San Diego: Harcourt Brace.
dePaola, Tomie. 1983. *The Legend of the Bluebonnet*. New York: G. P. Putnam's Sons.
dePaola, Tomie. 1988. *The Legend of the Indian Paintbrush*. New York: G. P. Putnam's Sons.
dePaola, Tomie. 1994. *The Legend of the Poinsettia*. New York: G. P. Putnam's Sons.
dePaola, Tomie. 1995. *Mary, the Mother of Jesus*. New York: Holiday House.
dePaola, Tomie. 2001. *Meet the Barkers*. New York: G. P. Putnam's Sons.
dePaola, Tomie. 1986. *Merry Christmas, Strega Nona*. San Diego, CA: Harcourt Brace.
dePaola, Tomie. 2002. *Nana Upstairs & Nana Downstairs*. New York: G. P. Putnam's Sons.
dePaola, Tomie. 2002. *A New Barker in the House*. New York: G. P. Putnam's Sons.
dePaola, Tomie. 1980. *The Night before Christmas*. New York: Holiday House.
dePaola, Tomie. 1981. *Now One Foot, Now the Other*. New York: G. P. Putnam's Sons.
dePaola, Tomie. 1979. *Oliver Button Is a Sissy*. San Diego, CA: Harcourt Brace.
dePaola, Tomie. 2001. *On My Way*. New York: G. P. Putnam's Sons.
dePaola, Tomie. 1978. *Pancakes for Breakfast*. San Diego, CA: Harcourt Brace.
dePaola, Tomie. 2004. *Pascual and the Kitchen Angels*. G. P. Putnam's Sons
dePaola, Tomie. 1992. *Patrick, Patron Saint of Ireland*. New York: Holiday House.
dePaola, Tomie. 1978. *The Popcorn Book*. San Diego, CA: Harcourt Brace.
dePaola, Tomie. 1977. *The Quicksand Book*. New York: Holiday House.
dePaola, Tomie. 1975. *Strega Nona*. New York: Simon & Schuster.
dePaola, Tomie. 1982. *Strega Nona's Magic Lessons*. San Diego, CA: Harcourt Brace.
dePaola, Tomie. 1993. *Strega Nona Meets Her Match*. New York: G. P. Putnam's Sons.
dePaola, Tomie. 1996. *Strega Nona: Her Story*. New York: G. P. Putnam's Sons.
dePaola, Tomie. 2003. *Things Will NEVER Be the Same*. New York: G. P. Putnam's Sons.
dePaola, Tomie. 1993. *Tom*. New York: G. P. Putnam's Sons.
dePaola, Tomie. 1988. *Tomie dePaola's Book of Poems*. New York: G. P. Putnam's Sons.
dePaola, Tomie. 1986. *Tomie dePaola's Favorite Nursery Tales*. New York: G. P. Putnam's Sons.
dePaola, Tomie. 1985. *Tomie dePaola's Mother Goose*. New York: G. P. Putnam's Sons.
dePaola, Tomie. 1989. *Tony's Bread*. New York: G. P. Putnam's Sons.
dePaola, Tomie. 2003. *Trouble in the Barker's Class*. New York: G. P. Putnam's Sons.
dePaola, Tomie. 1974. *Watch Out for the Chicken Feet in Your Soup*. Englewood Cliffs, NJ: Prentice-Hall.
dePaola, Tomie. 2002. *What a Year*. New York: G. P. Putnam's Sons.
dePaola, Tomie. 1966. *The Wonderful Dragon of Timlin*. Indianapolis, IN: Bob-Merrill.
Dunn, Susan, and Rob Larson. 1990. *Design Technology: Children's Engineering*. Briston, PA: Falmer Press, Taylor and Francis, Inc.
Durant, Penny Raife. 1994. *Bubblemania*. New York: Avon.

Egan, Robert. 1997. *From Wheat to Pasta*. New York: Children's Press.
Eldin, Peter. 1996. *The Most Excellent Book of How to Be a Magician with Easy Step-by-Step Instructions for a Brilliant Performance*. London: Aladdin/Watts.
Elleman, Barbara. 1999. *Tomie dePaola: His Art and His Stories*. New York: G. P. Putnam's Sons.
Esposito, Mary Ann. 1995. *Celebrations, Italian Style*. Illustrations by Tomie dePaola. New York: Hearst.
Feller, Ron, and Marsha Feller. 1985. *Paper Masks and Puppets for Stories, Songs, and Plays*. Seattle, WA: The Arts Factory.
Firth, Margaret. 2003. *Frida Kahlo: The Artist Who Painted Herself*. Illustrations by Tomie dePaola. New York: Grosset & Dunlap.
Graham, John. 1976. *I Love You, Mouse*. Illustrations by Tomie dePaola. San Diego, CA: Harcourt Brace.
Harbison, Elizabeth. 1997. *Loaves of Fun: A History of Bread with Activities and Recipes from around the World*. Chicago: Chicago Press Review.
Hart, Avery, and Paul Mantell. 1996. *Kids Garden! The Anytime, Anyplace Guide to Sowing & Growing Fun*. Charlotte, VT: Williamson.
International Reading Association. 1996. *Standards of the English Language Arts*. Newark, DE: IRA.
Johnson, Terry, and Daphne Louis. 1987. *Literacy through Literature*. Portsmouth, NH: Heinemann.
Johnston, Tony. 1995. *Alice Nizzy Nazzy, the Witch of Sante Fe*. Illustrations by Tomie dePaola. New York: G. P. Putnam's Sons.
Johnston, Tony. 1985. *The Quilt Story*. Illustrations by Tomie dePaola. New York: G. P. Putnam's Sons.
Johnston, Tony. 1983. *The Vanishing Pumpkin*. Illustrations by Tomie dePaola. New York: G. P. Putnam's Sons.
Kidstamps Rubber Stamp Company. PO Box 18699, Cleveland Heights, Ohio 44118.
Lattimore, Deborah Nourse. 1991. *The Sailor Who Captured the Sea: A Story of the Book of Kells*. New York: HarperCollins.
Levenson, George. 2004. *Bread Comes to Life: A Garden of Wheat and a Loaf to Eat*. Berkeley, CA: Tricycle Press.
Lukens, Rebecca J. 2002. *A Critical Handbook of Children's Literature*. New York: HarperCollins.
Meltzer, Milton. 1992. *The Amazing Potato: A Story in Which the Incas, Conquistadors, Marie Antoinette, Thomas Jefferson, Wars, Famines, Immigrants, and French Fries All Play a Part*. New York: HarperCollins.
Miller, Lisa. 1965. *Sound*. New York: Coward-McCann.
Moore, Clement. 1980. *The Night before Christmas*. Illustrations by Tomie dePaola. New York: Holiday House.
Norris, Kathleen. 2001. *The Holy Twins: Benedict and Scholastica*. Illustrations by Tomie dePaola. New York: G. P. Putnam's Sons.
Pomeroy, Diana. 1996. *One Potato: A Counting Book of Potato Prints*. San Diego: Harcourt Brace.
Prager, Annabelle. 1989. *The Spooky Halloween Party*. Illustrations by Tomie dePaola. New York: Random House.
Sapon-Shevin, Mara. 1998. *Because We Can Change the World: A Practical Guide to Building Cooperative, Inclusive Classroom Communities*. Boston, MA: Allyn & Bacon.

Strega Nona . . . and More Caldecott Award-Winning Folk Tales. 2004. New York: Scholastic. Videocassette or DVD.

A Visit with Tomie dePaola. Videocassette. 1996. Produced by Whitebird, Inc.

Yeats, William Butler. 1973. *Fairy and Folk Tales of Ireland.* New York: Macmillan.

Yopp, Ruth Helen, and Hallie Kay Yopp. 2001. *Literature-based Reading Activities.* Boston: Allyn & Bacon.

Zubrowski, Bernie, and Joan Drescher. 1979. *Bubbles: A Children's Museum Activity Book.* Boston: Little, Brown.

Index

Ads: before and after, 70; realty, 86
Ahlberg, Allan, 12
Ahlberg, Janet, 12
Alice Nizzy Nazzy, the Witch of Sante Fe (Johnston), 114
Aloe, 70
Alphabetizing, 11
The Amazing Potato: A Story in Which the Incas, Conquistadors, Marie Antoinette, Thomas Jefferson, Wars, Famines, Immigrants, and French Fries All Play a Part (Meltzer), 93
The Amazing Potato Book (Bourgeois), 92, 96
Andy, That's My Name, 1–5, 109, 114
Anticipation Guide, 10, 48
The Art Lesson, 8–14, 114, 120, 125, 127
Art Response, drawing and painting: from a bird's eye view, 58, 121; diptychs or triptychs, 122; family celebrations, 58; names, 4–5; *Stregas*, 37; warm up, 121
Art Response, masks: Bambolona, 52; Big Anthony/Antonia, 52; my ideal vacation, 76
Art Response, miscellaneous: before and after ads, 70; before and after cures, 70; crayon art activity book, 14; creating leprechauns, 95; design a new home for Fin or Oonagh, 86; design your own pooka, 99; display, 14; favorite art lesson, 13; found object boxes, 122; friendship blocks, 18–19; frying pan, 86; giant kids, 86; gift tags, 76; heart activities, 129; Irish, 86; Jamie O'Rourke mural, 95; leprechaun traps, 95; magic rings, 47; paper plate characters, 70; pasta, 39–41; photo collage, 30; Pookas on display, 99; pop-ups, 70; posters, 110; potato prints, 95, 129; self-portraits, 14, 109; sharing art ideas, 13; shrines, 122; silhouettes, 27; special treasures, 27; Starring!, 7; think big, 85; time capsules, 17; travel poster critique, 76; warm-up drawings and paintings, 121. See also Ads; Cards; Mural; Puppets
Author study, 125
Autobiographical books, 1–31, 114, 125

Baby Poems, 29
The Baby Sister, 28–31, 114, 118
Bare feet math, 18–20
The *Barker* series, 114, 132, 134
Barney and Friends, 118
Because We Can Change the World: A Practical Guide to Building Cooperative, Inclusive Classroom Communities (Sapon-Shevin), 8
Bet You Can! Science Possibilities to Fool You (Cobb and Darling), 64
Bet You Can't! Science Impossibilities to Fool You (Cobb and Darling), 64
Big Anthony and the Magic Ring, 43–48. See also Mural; Puppet play; Puppets; Role-playing
Big Anthony: His Story, 71–74. See also Mural; Puppet play; Puppets; Role-playing
Bill and Pete, 101–104, 114; friendship web, 103; K-W-L, 101; mural, 109
Bill and Pete Go Down the Nile, 104–107, 114; create a safety manual, 105–106; design a field trip, 105; mural, 109
Bill and Pete to the Rescue, 107–111, 114; mural, 109
Biographer, 65, 71
Biography, 71; writing, 69
Bird's eye view, 58, 121
The Book of Kells, 86, 87

Index

Books: giant, 85; making, 17; parts of, 66; timeline accordion books, 67
Bourgeois, Paulette, 92
Box It or Bag It Math (Burke, Snider, and Symonds), 126
Bread: baking, 53, 127; balancing, 54; dolls, 26, 42; graph, 52–53; history of, 53; inviting bakers to speak, 53; touring factory, 53; video, 53
Bread Comes to Life: A Garden of Wheat and a Loaf to Eat (Levenson), 53
Brownlie, Fay, 84–85
Bubble: science, 77–78, 129; story, 78; wish bubbles, 129
The Bubble Factory, 78, 129
Bubblemania (Durant), 78, 129
Bubbles: A Children's Museum Activity Book (Zubrowski and Drescher), 78
Bullies, discussing, 81
Burke, Donna, 126

Caldecott Medal, 35
Cards, 25
Career Day, 69
Carlson, Laurie, 59
Cassidy, John, 78, 129
Celebrations, Italian Style (Esposito), 42
Celtic music, 87
Chamomile, 70
Chants, songs, 46
Character: descriptions, 13; display, 92; paper plate, 70
Charney, Ruth, 8
Chicken: feet, 22; soup graph, 27
Child Development Project, 8
Christopher, The Holy Giant, 132
Class meetings, 8, 98
Close, Susan, 84–85
The Cloud Book, 114, 131
The Clown of God, 131
Cobb, Vicki, 64
Collage, 30, 68
Community building, 1, 8, 59, 98
Cook, Deanna, 42
Cookies, baking, 127, 129
Cooking: baking, 53; bread, 26; bread dolls, 26, 42; bread graph, 52–53; Donna Chiara's Stelline d'Oro, 42; Family Traditions Cookbook, 56; popcorn, 126; potato recipe book, 92; potatoes, 126. *See also* Cooking; Pasta; Potatoes
Country Angel Christmas, 115, 131
Crayons, 11–12; activity book, 14; alphabetizing, 11; art ideas, 127; Crayola, 8
A Critical Handbook of Children's Literature (Lukens), 82–83, 88
Cultures: experiencing, 25–26; graphing, 26; writing about, 13
Cures, 70. *See also* Remedies

Dance, tarantella, 47
Darling, Kathy, 64
Davies, Valentine, 131
Dedication page, 66
dePaola, Tomie: author study, 125; birthday card, sending, 120; Day, 125; home, 113; just like…18; studio, 113; warm-up drawings and paintings, 121
Design Technology: Children's Engineering (Dunn and Larson), 64
Diptychs and triptychs, painting and drawing, 122
Distractions, 72
Donna Chiara's Stelline d'Oro, 42
Drama: sharing family activities, 27; Special Person Day, 46; talent show, 8. *See also* Puppet Plays; Puppets; Role Playing.
Dreams, 75
Drescher, Joan, 78
Dunn, Susan, 64
Durant, Penny Raife, 78, 129

An Early American Christmas, 131
Echinecea, 70
ECOART! Earth-Friendly Art & Craft Experiences for 3–9-year-olds (Carlson), 59
Eldin, Peter, 54
Esposito, Mary Ann, 42

The Family Christmas Tree Book, 115
Family Traditions Cookbook, 56
Feller, Marsha, 52
Feller, Ron, 52
Field trip, 105–106
Fin M'Coul, the Giant of Knockmany Hill, 79–87
Folktale: checklist, 88; common elements of, 83–84; writing, 82

Footprints, 20
Footwear, creating, 18
Found object boxes, 122
Francis, Poor Man of Assisi, 132
Frida's Table, 118, 121
The Friendly Beasts, 131
Friendship: blocks, 18–19; poems, 104; riddles, 104; thank-you notes, 104; web, 103

Geography, 34, 74, 104
Gift tags, creating, 76
Grandparents, 14–17, 20–27
Graphing: bath or shower, 77–78; bread, 52; chicken soup, 27; holidays, 25–26; human, 30; pasta sauce, 41; December celebrations, 55

Handwriting, 104
Harbison, Elizabeth, 53
Hart, Avery, 71
Heart: activities, 129; Tomie dePaola trademark, 116
Herbs, 70–71
Here We All Are, 131
The Holy Twins: Benedict and Scholastica (Norris), 132

Integrated Language Arts: alphabetizing, 11; character display, 92; class recipe book, 92; collage, 68; comparing Nona and Amelia, 67; creating business cards, 61; creating handbills, 61; distractions, 72; dreams, 75; falling stars, 24; home interiors, 64; interviews, 11, 21; name activities, 3; pantomime, 11; posters, 51; potatoes, 91–92; reference skills, 108; retelling, 35; rewriting endings, 36; special times, 24; *Strega* or *Stregone* business, 61; timeline accordion book, 67; timelines, 51. *See also* Crayons; Reader's theatre; Reference skills; Stories; Storytelling
Interviews, 11, 21, 69
Italian landmarks, finding, 74
Irish: dialect and word fun, 90; music, 87; stories, 79; words and phrases, 82

Jamie O'Rourke and the Big Potato, 87–95, 99, 126; character display, 92; K-W-L, 87; leprechauns, 90, 95; mural, 95; songs, 91. *See also* Potatoes

Jamie O'Rourke and the Pooka, 79, 95–99; design your own pooka, 99; Pookas on Parade, 99
Jingle, the Christmas Clown, 42, 127, 131
Job, application, 73
Jobs, odd, 73
Johnson, Terry, 111
Jokes, practical, 22
The Jolly Postman, or Other People's Letters (Ahlberg), 82

Kahlo, Frida, 58, 118
The Kids' Cat Book, 114, 131
Kid's Garden! The Anytime, Anyplace Guide to Sowing & Growing Fun (Hart and Avery), 71
The Kid's Multicultural Cookbook (Cook), 42, 127
Kidstamps Rubber Stamp Co., 37
K-W-L: Bill and Pete, 101; Jamie O'Rourke, 87, 90; Tomie dePaola, 115

The Lady of Guadalupe, 132
Larson, Rob, 64
Lattimore, Deborah Nourse, 87
The Legend of Bluebonnet, 115, 131
The Legend of Old Befana, 119
The Legend of the Indian Paintbrush, 115, 131
The Legend of the Pointsettia, 115, 131
Leprechauns, 79, 87, 90, 95
Letters: reference, 73; thank you, 17; writing, 90, 98
Levenson, George, 53
Literacy through Literature (Johnson and Louis), 111
Literature-based Reading Activities (Yopp and Yopp), 81
Loaves of Fun: A History of Bread with Activities and Recipes from around the World (Harbison), 53
Louis, Daphne, 111
Lukens, Rebecca, 82–83, 88

Magic: hats, 64; rings, 47, tricks, 54
Mantell, Paul, 71
Maps: semantic, 79–81; using, 115
Mary, the Mother of Jesus, 132
Math activities: bare feet, 18–20; measuring pasta, 43; weighing pasta, 43. *See also* Graphing

Meet the Barkers, 132
Meltzer, Milton, 93, 96
Merry Christmas, Strega Nona, 54–59, 76; Family Traditions Cookbook, 55. *See also* Mural; Puppet Plays; Puppets; Reader's theatre; Role-playing
Mint, 70
Miracle on 34th Street (Davies), 131
The Most Excellent Book of How to Be a Magician with Easy Step-by-Step Instructions for a Brilliant Performance (Eldin), 54
Mr. Potato Head, 92
Mural: *Big Anthony and the Magic Ring*, 47; *Big Anthony: His Story*, 74; giant, 85; *Merry Christmas, Strega Nona*, 58; New Orleans, 109; Nile River area, 109; *Strega Nona*, 38; *Strega Nona: Her Story*, 69; *Strega Nona Meets Her Match*, 62; *Strega Nona Takes a Vacation*, 76; *Strega Nona's Magic Lessons*, 52

Names, activities, 1–5
Nana Upstairs & Nana Downstairs, 22–23, 114, 120
A New Barker in the House, 132
New Orleans, 108–109
The Night before Christmas, 115, 119, 131
Nile River, 103, 108–109
Norris, Kathleen, 132
Now One Foot, Now the Other, 14–21, 114, 117; block design activity, 18–19

Olive oil, 46, 48
Oliver Button Is a Sissy, 6–8, 114
One Potato: A Counting Book of Potato Prints (Pomeroy), 95
On My Way, 131

Painting. *See* Art Response
Pancakes, making, 127
Pancakes for Breakfast, 127
Pantomime, 11
Paper Masks and Puppets for Stories, Songs and Plays (Feller and Feller), 52
Paper plate characters, 70
Pascual and the Kitchen Angels, 132
Pasta: art, 39–41; chart, 41; cooking, 41, 127; graphing, 41; how it is made, 42; math, 42–43

Patrick, Patron Saint of Ireland, 132
Pledges, 8
Poetry: acrostic, 4; baby poems, 29; friendship, 104
Point of view, 17, 61, 82
Pomeroy, Diana, 95
Pookas, 95–99
The Popcorn Book, 114, 119, 126, 131
Popeye, 117, 127–28
Pop-ups, 70
Portraitist, 65
Portraits, 70. *See also* Self-portraits
Posters, 51, 76, 110
Potatoes: and people, 92; background, 96; baking, 126; nutrition, 93; planting, 93; prints, 95; recipes, 92; science, 93–95; sorting, 93
Prager, Annabelle, 115
Prequel, 65
Pre-reading Activities: anticipation guide, 9, 49; before there were doctors, 34; experiencing other cultures, 25–26; portraitist, what is, 65; prequel, sharing, 65; questionnaire, 6; semantic maps, 79–81; special person for the day, 43–44; spring fever stories, 44; what is a biographer? 65; what is a pooka? 97. *See also*: Geography
Puppets: *Big Anthony and the Magic Ring*, 46–47; *Big Anthony: His Story*, 74; *Fin M'Coul*, 85; *Merry Christmas, Strega Nona*, 58; *Strega Nona*, 38, 40; *Strega Nona: Her Story*, 69; *Strega Nona Meets Her Match*, 62; *Strega Nona Takes a Vacation*, 77; *Strega Nona's Magic Lessons*, 52; Puppet Play. *See* Puppets

The Quicksand Book, 114, 131
The Quilt Story (Johnston), 117

Reader's theatre, 11, 37; *Fin M'Coul*, 85; *Merry Christmas, Strega Nona*, 58; *Strega Nona*, 37
Recipe: book, 92; pasta sauce, 42; potato, 92
Reference: ideas, 107; skills, 102–103, 108
Research, 104, 108
Rings: magic, 47; removing, 46
Role-playing: *Strega Nona: Her Story*, 69; *Strega Nona Meets Her Match*, 62; *Strega Nona Takes a Vacation*, 77

Safety manual, creating, 105
The Sailor Who Captured the Sea: A Story of the Book of Kells (Lattimore), 87
Sapon-Shevin, Mara, 8
Science: bubble, 78; chicken feet, 22; endangered species, 108; experiments, 64; herbs, 70–71; olive oil, 48; potato, 93–96
Secret pals, 59
Self-portraits, 14, 70, 109
Semantic maps, 79–81
Senses, 16, 20, 82
Shrines, 118, 122
Siblings, 28–31
Snider, Allyn, 126
Songs, chants, 69, 91
Speaking bubbles, 84–85, 93
The Spooky Halloween Party (Prager), 115
Stars, falling, 24
Stories: an old saying, 17; point of view, 17; recording, 22; taping, 17. *See also* Writing
Storytelling, 21–22
Strega Nona, 33–43, 71, 90, 113–114, 119, 127; rubber stamps, 37. *See also* Mural; Puppet Play; Puppets; Role-playing
Strega Nona: Her Story, 65–71. *See also* Mural; Puppet Play; Puppets; Role-playing
Strega Nona Meets Her Match, 60–64; Big Anthony's healing ways, 63–64; business cards, 61; Strega business, 61. *See also* Mural; Puppet Play; Puppets; Role-playing
Strega Nona Takes a Vacation, 74–78. *See also* Mural; Puppet Play; Puppets; Role-playing
Strega Nona's Magic Lessons, 48–54, 119. *See also* Mural; Puppet Play; Puppets; Role-playing
Symonds, Paula, 126

Teaching Children to Care (Charney), 8
Temptations, writing about, 76
Things Will NEVER Be the Same, 132
Thinking bubbles, 84–85
Thyme, 70
Time capsules, 17
Timeline: bread, 51
Timeline accordion books, 67–68
Title page, 66

Tom, 20–22, 114, 119
Tomie dePaola's Book of Poems, 115
Tomie dePaola's Favorite Nursery Tales, 115
Tomie dePaola's Mother Goose, 115
Tomorrow's Classroom Today: Strategies for Creating Active Readers, Writers and Thinkers (Brownlie, Close, and Wingren), 84–85
Tony's Bread, 127
Trouble in the Barker's Class, 132
26 Fairmount Avenue, 1

The Unbelievable Bubble Book (Cassidy), 78, 129

Vacations, 76
The Vanishing Pumpkin (Johnston), 115
Venn diagram, 67
A Visit with Tomie dePaola, 37, 58, 113–123, 125–127
Vocabulary, 102–103, 107

Wanna Bet? Science Challenges to Fool You (Cobb and Darling), 64
Watch Out for the Chicken Feet in Your Soup, 25–27, 42, 114, 120, 127
Ways We Want Our Class to Be: Class Meetings That Build Commitment to Kindness and Learning (Child Development Project), 8
Web, creating, 44; friendship, 103
What a Year, 132
Wingren, Linda, 84–85
Writing: cards, 25, 36, 126; character descriptions, 13; diary entries, 16; dreams, 75; endings, 36, 73, 82; excuses, 57; folktales, 82; giant postcards, 82; interviews, 69, 75; job application, 73; letters, 17, 62, 73, 90, 98, 104; lists, 57, 73, 76, 90, 98; love notes, 109; news flash, 109; personal events, 36; pledges, 8; poems, 22, 104; point of view, 17, 61, 82, 90; practical jokes, 22; remedies, 46, 63–64; riddles, 104; stories: 16–17, 24, 45–46, 103, 126

Yopp, Hallie Kay, 81
Yopp, Ruth Helen, 81

Zubrowski, Bernie, 78

About the Author

Val Hornburg has taught for the past 25 years in both public and private elementary schools. She has known Tomie dePaolo for over 20 years and is deeply honored that he has endorsed this work. She has her M.A.T. degree with a reading endorsement from Lewis & Clark College in Portland, Oregon.

Val has won the nationally prestigious Miriam Joseph Farrell Award for Outstanding Teaching. Val lives with her husband, Bill Zuelke, and daughter Noelle, in Portland, Oregon.